180 Days of
Spelling & Word Study
for Third Grade

Author

Shireen Pesez Rhoades, M.A.Ed.

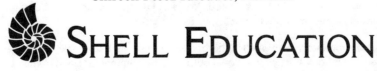

SHELL EDUCATION

Publishing Credits

Corinne Burton, M.A.Ed., *Publisher*
Conni Medina, M.A.Ed., *Editor in Chief*
Emily R. Smith, M.A.Ed., *Content Director*
Véronique Bos, *Creative Director*
Shaun N. Bernadou, *Art Director*
Lynette Ordoñez, *Editor*
Bianca Marchese, M.S.Ed., *Editor*
Jess Johnson, *Graphic Designer*
Dani Neiley, *Assistant Editor*

Image Credits

All images are from iStock and/or Shutterstock.

Standards

© 2014 Mid-continent Research for Education and Learning
© Copyright 2010. National Governors Association Center for Best Practices and Council of Chief State School Officers.
All rights reserved.
© Copyright 2007–2018 Texas Education Agency (TEA). All rights reserved.
© 2007 Teachers of English to Speakers of Other Languages, Inc. (TESOL)
© 2014 Board of Regents of the University of Wisconsin System, on behalf of WIDA— www.wida.us.

Shell Education

A division of Teacher Created Materials
5301 Oceanus Drive
Huntington Beach, CA 92649-1030
www.tcmpub.com/shell-education

ISBN 978-1-4258-3311-4
©2019 Shell Educational Publishing, Inc.

Table of Contents

Introduction

180 Days of Spelling and Word Study provides the missing piece to today's language arts curriculum. Developed by a reading consultant with more than 20 years of classroom and literacy experience, this research-based program is easy to implement, simple to differentiate, and adaptable to any instructional model. The activities are straightforward and engaging. Most importantly, they address today's college and career readiness standards.

This book boosts students' spelling, vocabulary, and decoding skills by familiarizing them with common patterns in a logical, sequential format. Each five-day unit explores a new concept or letter pattern.

Goals of the Series

The first goal of the series is to build students' familiarity with common spelling patterns and rules. The scope and sequence has been designed using a developmental approach, taking into account students' predictive stages of spelling development. Units progress from basic letter sounds to challenging patterns and spiral from one year to the next.

A second goal is to strengthen decoding skills. When students spend a week or more immersed in a particular phonetic pattern, they start to notice and apply the pattern to their daily reading. This program's emphasis on common spelling patterns strengthens students' word-attack skills and helps them break large words into syllables and meaningful chunks.

Introduction *(cont.)*

Goals of the Series *(cont.)*

Vocabulary development is the third, and perhaps most critical, goal of the series. Tasks are meaning-based, so students cannot complete them successfully without some knowledge of the words' definitions or parts of speech. Additionally, activities are designed to deepen students' knowledge of targeted words by requiring them to manipulate synonyms, antonyms, and multiple meanings.

Structured Practice

To be successful in spelling, students must focus on the words, word parts, patterns, and definitions. For that reason, this series uses structured practice. Rather than changing the activities week-to-week, the daily activities are repeated throughout the 36 units. That way, students can focus on the words instead of learning how to complete the activities.

The following activities are used throughout this book:

Title of Activity	Description
Analogies	Students use a word bank to complete analogies.
Homophones	Students choose the correct homophones to complete sentences.
Inflectional Endings	Students add inflectional endings to given words.
Prefixes and Suffixes	Students add prefixes or suffixes to given words. Then, they use the new words to complete sentences.
Sentence Completions	Students use a word bank to complete sentences.
Sentence Types	Students use given words to write statements, questions, and exclamations.
Synonyms and Antonyms	Students use a word bank to list synonyms or antonyms of given words.
Turn the Question Around	Students use given words to answer questions in complete sentences. *Turn the Question Around* means restating the question in the answer.
Word Sorts	Students sort words into two categories.

How to Use This Book

180 Days of Spelling and Word Study is comprised of 36 units. Each unit revolves around a particular phonetic pattern and includes five separate activities. They can be assigned as homework or morning work, or they can be used as part of a word work rotation. Activities vary throughout each unit.

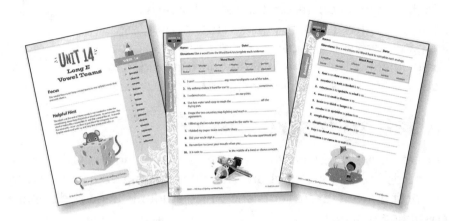

In this book, students will explore: long and short vowels, vowel teams, diphthongs, digraphs, hard/soft consonants, and *r*-controlled vowels. Students apply these patterns to two-syllable words with prefixes and predictable endings, such as *–ic*, *–ish*, and *–le*. Students begin to explore unusual vowel teams and the many roles of the silent *e*. Common prefixes, suffixes, and homophones are studied as well.

Unit Assessments

A list of words is provided at the beginning of each unit. The words share a phonetic pattern that is reinforced in activities throughout the unit. You may choose to send the words home as part of a traditional study list. Additional spelling activities are provided on page 7. These activities can be specifically assigned, or the whole list can be sent home as a school-home connection.

However, in place of a typical spelling test, you are encouraged to administer the unit quizzes provided on pages 237–238. Each unit quiz contains two words and a dictation sentence. The individual words fit the unit pattern but have not been previously studied. Spelling the words correctly demonstrates that students have mastered the unit's spelling objectives and can apply them to daily work. Further, two to four words in the sentence dictation come from the study list. The rest of the sentence consists of high-frequency or review words. Dictation sentences measure how well students can spell target words in context, while attending to capitalization and punctuation rules.

Unit Assessments *(cont.)*

The units are grouped into categories so you can diagnose how well students understand key phonetic patterns. By grouping these units together in this way, you can record the scores for each unit's assessment within a category and better assess student progress. See the Spelling Categories chart on page 239. You may also choose to record unit assessment scores in the Analysis Charts provided in the Digital Resources. See page 240 for more information.

Differentiating Instruction

Once a phonetic category's assessment results are gathered and analyzed, use the results to inform the way you differentiate instruction. The data can help determine which phonetic patterns are the most difficult for students and which students need additional instructional support and continued practice.

Whole-Class Support

The results of the diagnostic analysis may show that the entire class is struggling with certain phonetic patterns. If they have been taught in the past, this indicates that further instruction or reteaching is necessary. If these patterns have not been taught in the past, this data is a great preassessment and may demonstrate that students do not have a working knowledge of the weekly pattern. Thus, careful planning for reintroducing the words or patterns may be required.

Small-Group or Individual Support

The results of the diagnostic analysis may also show that an individual student or a small group of students is struggling with certain spelling patterns. If these patterns have been taught in the past, this indicates that further instruction or reteaching is necessary. Consider pulling these students aside to instruct them further while others are working independently. Students may also benefit from extra practice using spelling games or computer-based resources.

You can also use the results to help identify proficient individual students or groups of students who are ready for enrichment or above-level spelling instruction. These students may benefit from independent learning contracts or more challenging words. The Additional Spelling Activities chart has strong options to further challenge students (page 7 and in the Digital Resources).

Included in the Digital Resources are lists of words used in *180 Days of Spelling and Word Study* for grades 2 and 4. These lists can be used for differentiation.

How to Use This Book *(cont.)*

Additional Spelling Activities

The activities included here offer additional ways to practice the spelling words in each unit. They also make a great school-home connection!

Activity Name	Description
ABC Order	Write each word on a separate slip of paper. Mix up the slips of paper, and arrange them in ABC order.
Air Spelling	Spell each word in the air using one or two fingers. Have a partner guess which word you spelled.
Best Writing	Write each spelling word two times in your best printing or cursive.
Cut Out Words	Cut out letters from newspapers or magazines, and use the letters to form the spelling words. Glue the words onto a sheet of paper.
Mnemonic Sentences	Write a mnemonic sentence for each spelling word. For example, a sentence for the word *first* could be: *Fred is racing scooters tomorrow*.
Rainbow Spelling	Write each word with a crayon. Trace around the words in a different color crayon. Trace around both colors in a third color.
Silly Spelling Story	Write a silly story with a beginning, middle, and end that uses as many spelling words as possible.
Spelling Charades	Act out a spelling word. The first person to correctly guess and spell the word gets to act out the next word.
Spelling Hangman	Create a sentence using two or more spelling words. Play hangman until another person solves the puzzle.
Spelling Poem	Write a poem using as many spelling words as possible.
Spelling Scramble	Write each spelling word on a separate index card. Cut apart the letters of each word. Place the letters for each word in a separate zip-top bag. Working with a partner, dump out the letters from one bag at a time and unscramble the words.

How to Use This Book (cont.)

Word Lists

This chart lists the words and phonetic patterns covered in each unit.

Unit	Words	Spelling Pattern
1	apple, attic, battle, candle, classic, fabric, glasses, handle, paddle, plastic, saddle, sample, taxes, traffic, vanish	short *a* words
2	brittle, build, dishes, finish, giggle, griddle, kisses, little, middle, mixes, picnic, scribble, simple, sizzle, wiggle	short *i* words
3	bread, breath, dresses, health, heavy, meddle, medic, pebble, ready, relish, selfish, settle, spread, thread, weather	short *e* words
4	bottle, boxes, comic, foxes, gobble, goggles, hobble, nozzle, optic, polish, topic, topple, toxic, tropic, wobble	short *o* words
5	bubble, country, couple, cover, double, front, jungle, money, month, public, publish, punish, puzzle, touch, trouble	short *u* words
6	bucket, buckle, chuckle, crackle, freckles, hockey, jacket, jockey, nickel, pickle, pocket, rocket, socket, tackle, ticket	*ck* pattern
7	assign, bristle, bustle, castle, climb, design, hustle, knuckle, nestle, resign, rustle, sign, whistle, wrestle, wriggle	silent letters
8	decade, delete, excuse, exhale, explode, include, invite, mistake, paste, promote, propose, provide, refuse, taste, waste	silent *e* words
9	chance, dance, decide, device, excite, fancy, fence, glance, once, precise, prince, produce, recite, reduce, since	soft *c* words
10	bridge, change, cringe, gentle, guest, guide, guilty, guy, judge, magic, pledge, plunge, sponge, tragic, trudge	soft and hard *g* words
11	catch, crutches, enough, graphics, laugh, phonics, rough, scratch, sketch, snatch, stitches, stretch, tough, trophy, witch	consonant digraphs
12	able, baby, basic, craters, crazy, fable, gravy, ladle, lady, later, lazy, paper, stable, staple, table	long *a* words
13	afraid, betray, delay, details, eight, exclaim, explain, freight, holiday, praise, raise, sleigh, veil, veins, weigh	long *a* vowel teams
14	breathe, breeze, cheese, crease, freeze, grease, lease, leave, peace, please, sleeve, sneeze, squeeze, weave, wheeze	long *e* vowel teams
15	agree, asleep, beetle, beneath, between, ceiling, deceive, eagle, easy, either, needle, people, receive, steeple, weird	more long *e* vowel teams
16	apply, buy, deny, dial, icy, July, lightning, rely, reply, slimy, spider, supply, tiger, title, trial	long *i* vowel team and open syllables
17	below, bowl, elbow, follow, grown, hollow, meadow, mellow, pillow, rainbow, shadow, shallow, widow, window, yellow	long *o* vowel team
18	bony, boulder, dough, ghost, hotel, noble, poll, program, robot, scroll, shoulder, smoky, stroll, though, toll	long *o* patterns

How to Use This Book *(cont.)*

Unit	Words	Spelling Pattern
19	bruise, choose, cruel, cruise, fuel, group, juice, loose, lose, move, prove, route, soup, through, truth	long *u* patterns
20	argue, balloon, bugle, cartoon, duty, improve, music, nephew, noodle, pursue, recruit, remove, rescue, shampoo, value	more long *u* patterns
21	bulge, collapse, collide, combine, compete, complete, contain, contrast, control, convince, could've, insult, pulse, result, should've	schwa sound
22	allow, amount, blouse, bounce, chowder, devour, discount, drowsy, hourly, house, mouse, pounce, scrounge, shower, spouse	*ou/ow* diphthongs
23	annoy, appoint, avoid, choice, deploy, destroy, employ, enjoy, foyer, joyful, loiter, noise, oily, rejoice, voice	*oi/oy* diphthongs
24	autumn, caught, cause, daughter, false, gauze, launch, laundry, naughty, pause, sauce, swallow, taught, waffle, water	*au/aw* digraphs
25	across, bossy, bought, broad, brought, cough, fought, frolic, frosty, lacrosse, offer, often, ought, thought, trough	/aw/ pattern with *ough* and *oa*
26	army, artist, farther, garlic, garnish, guard, hardly, heart, large, marble, partner, party, remark, sparkle, tardy	*r*-controlled vowels with *ar*
27	aware, barely, beware, careful, declare, fare, glare, pare, prepare, rare, scary, share, spare, square, stare	long *a* patterns with *are*
28	airplane, bear, dairy, despair, fairground, fairy, impair, pear, prairie, repair, staircase, swear, tear, wear, wheelchair	long *a* patterns with *air* and *ear*
29	acorn, border, forty, import, morning, northern, order, perform, popcorn, record, reform, report, stormy, story, transport	*r*-controlled vowels with *or*
30	board, course, court, divorce, door, enforce, explore, floor, force, horse, ignore, poor, roar, soar, source	*r*-controlled vowels with *oar, oor, our, ore*
31	quart, quarter, war, ward, warm, warn, wart, work, world, worm, worry, worse, worst, worth, worthless	*r*-controlled vowels with *quar, war, wor*
32	alert, danger, desert, every, germs, merge, nerve, never, pattern, prefer, reverse, serve, stranger, swerve, verse	*r*-controlled vowels with *er*
33	blurry, cure, curse, curve, disturb, during, hurry, nurse, pure, purple, purse, sturdy, surprise, turtle, urge	*r*-controlled vowels with *ur*
34	birthday, circle, dirty, early, earn, earth, firmly, heard, learn, pearl, rehearse, search, thirsty, thirty, yearn	*r*-controlled vowels with *ear* and *ir*
35	action, auction, caption, caution, fiction, fraction, lotion, mention, motion, nation, option, potion, question, section, station	*–tion* ending
36	among, angle, angry, ankle, belong, finger, hanger, hungry, longest, pinkish, single, sprinkle, stronger, wrinkle, young	*ng* and *nk* patterns

Standards Correlations

Shell Education is committed to producing educational materials that are research and standards based. All products are correlated to the academic standards of all 50 states, the District of Columbia, the Department of Defense Dependent Schools, and the Canadian provinces.

How to Find Standards Correlations

To print a customized correlation report of this product for your state, visit **www.tcmpub.com/ administrators/correlations/** and follow the online directions. If you require assistance in printing correlation reports, please contact the Customer Service Department at 1-877-777-3450.

Purpose and Intent of Standards

The Every Student Succeeds Act (ESSA) mandates that all states adopt challenging academic standards that help students meet the goal of college and career readiness. While many states already adopted academic standards prior to ESSA, the act continues to hold states accountable for detailed and comprehensive standards.

Standards are designed to focus instruction and guide adoption of curricula. Standards are statements that describe the criteria necessary for students to meet specific academic goals. They define the knowledge, skills, and content students should acquire at each level. Standards are also used to develop standardized tests to evaluate students' academic progress. Teachers are required to demonstrate how their lessons meet state standards. State standards are used in the development of all Shell products, so educators can be assured they meet the academic requirements of each state.

College and Career Readiness

In this book, the following college and career readiness (CCR) standards are met: Uses conventional spelling for high-frequency and other studied words and for adding suffixes to base words; uses spelling patterns and generalizations; and consults reference materials, including beginning dictionaries, as needed to check and correct spellings.

McREL Compendium

Each year, McREL analyzes state standards and revises the compendium to produce a general compilation of national standards. In this book, the following standard is met: Uses conventions of spelling in written compositions.

TESOL and WIDA Standards

In this book, the following English language development standards are met: Standard 1: English language learners communicate for social and instructional purposes within the school setting; Standard 2: English language learners communicate information, ideas, and concepts necessary for academic success in the content area of language arts.

UNIT 1
Short A Words

Focus

This week's focus is on short *a*, primarily two-syllable words with closed syllables.

Helpful Hint

Some of the words in this list are plurals. When a word ends with –*ch*, –*sh*, –*s*, –*x*, or –*z*, add –*es* to the end of the word instead of –*s* to make the word plural (glass → glasses; tax → taxes).

- apple
- attic
- battle
- candle
- classic
- fabric
- glasses
- handle
- paddle
- plastic
- saddle
- sample
- taxes
- traffic
- vanish

See page 7 for additional spelling activities.

Sentence Completions

Name: _____ Date: _____

Directions: Use a word from the Word Bank to complete each sentence.

Word Bank					
apple	attic	candle	classic	fabric	glasses
handle	paddle	plastic	sample	taxes	traffic

1. Can I _____ the peppermint ice cream to see if I like it?

2. Mom used a piece of red _____ to make my superhero cape.

3. I can't turn the _____ . The door must be locked!

4. Aniyah only needs to wear _____ when she's reading.

5. You can use these matches to light the _____ .

6. If we didn't pay _____ , there would be no money for police or schools.

7. The jar is made of _____ , so it won't shatter if you drop it.

8. Let's leave early in case there's a lot of _____ on the highway.

9. You can rest in the front of the canoe while I _____ across the lake.

10. Would you like a slice of _____ pie or pumpkin pie?

Name: _____ **Date:** _____

Directions: Use a word from the Word Bank to complete each section.

Synonyms and Antonyms

Word Bank					
apple	attic	battle	candle	classic	fabric
handle	paddle	plastic	saddle	sample	vanish

Write a synonym for each word.

1. cloth _____

2. combat _____

3. oar _____

4. knob _____

Write an antonym for each word.

5. basement _____

6. large helping _____

7. modern _____

8. appear _____

Write a word that fits each category.

9. orange, banana, cherry, _____

10. stirrups, reins, bridle, _____

11. wood, metal, cardboard, _____

12. lamp, sun, flashlight, _____

Name: _____ **Date:**_____

Directions: Study each example. Write a sentence for each word. End each sentence with the same punctuation as the example.

QUESTION

Ex. *close*:   Did you remember to *close* the door?

1. *attic*: _____

_____

2. *fabric*: _____

_____

STATEMENT

Ex. *note*:   I wrote a thank you *note* to my friend.

3. *plastic*: _____

_____

4. *glasses*: _____

_____

EXCLAMATION

Ex. *bone*:   I found a dinosaur *bone* in my backyard!

5. *handle*: _____

_____

6. *traffic*: _____

_____

Name: _____ **Date:** _____

Directions: Study how the word changes when you add new endings. Add the same endings to each word to create new words.

1. **wax**   waxes   waxing   waxed

   tax   _____   _____   _____

2. **saddle**   saddles   saddling   saddled

   paddle   _____   _____   _____

3. **trample**   tramples   trampling   trampled

   sample   _____   _____   _____

Directions: Find three words in the Word Bank related to each of the spelling words. Write the words on the correct lines.

Word Bank					
candles	handlebars	vanishes	battleship	candlestick	handles
candlelight	vanishing	vanished	handled	battles	battlefield

4. battle   _____   _____   _____

5. handle   _____   _____   _____

6. candle   _____   _____   _____

7. vanish   _____   _____   _____

28631—180 Days of Spelling and Word Study   15

Inflectional Endings

Analogies

Name: _____ **Date:** _____

Directions: Use a word from the Word Bank to complete each analogy.

Word Bank					
apple	attic	candle	classic	fabric	glasses
handle	paddle	plastic	saddle	taxes	traffic

1. **hear** is to **hearing aid** as **see** is to _____

2. **bike** is to **pedal** as **kayak** is to _____

3. **vegetable** is to **carrot** as **fruit** is to _____

4. **people** is to **mob** as **cars** is to _____

5. **cardstock** is to **paper** as **silk** is to _____

6. **balloon** is to **string** as **suitcase** is to _____

7. **new** is to **modern** as **old** is to _____

8. **clay** is to **bowl** as **wax** is to _____

9. **bicycle** is to **seat** as **horse** is to _____

10. **earn** is to **paycheck** as **pay** is to _____

UNIT 2
Short I Words

Focus

This week's focus is on short *i*, two-syllable words with closed syllables.

Helpful Hint

Most of the words on this list begin with a closed syllable (consonant-vowel-consonant or vowel-consonant). When breaking the words into parts, split them after the closed syllable. This means they will usually be divided between double letters or two consonants (*wig·gle*, *sim·ple*, *pic·nic*).

- ➤ **brittle**
- ➤ **build**
- ➤ **dishes**
- ➤ **finish**
- ➤ **giggle**
- ➤ **griddle**
- ➤ **kisses**
- ➤ **little**
- ➤ **middle**
- ➤ **mixes**
- ➤ **picnic**
- ➤ **scribble**
- ➤ **simple**
- ➤ **sizzle**
- ➤ **wiggle**

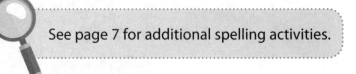

See page 7 for additional spelling activities.

Name: _____ **Date:** _____

Directions: Use a word from the Word Bank to complete each sentence.

Word Bank					
build	dishes	finish	giggle	griddle	kisses
little	middle	picnic	scribble	simple	sizzle

1. I prefer to sit in the _____ of the theater, not the front or back rows.

2. I hope we can _____ reading the story before recess.

3. Please write neatly. Don't just _____ on the paper.

4. My sister and I love to _____ sandcastles at the beach.

5. The bacon strips will _____ when you put them in the hot pan.

6. When I was _____ , I couldn't ride a bike without training wheels.

7. Dad cooked up some pancakes on the _____ .

8. Grandma always blows _____ when she drops me off at school.

9. This looks like a _____ project. There are only three steps to follow.

10. Please rinse all the cups and _____ and leave them on the counter.

Sentence Completions

Name: _____   Date:_____

Directions: Use a word from the Word Bank to complete each section.

Word Bank					
brittle	build	dishes	finish	giggle	kisses
little	middle	mixes	simple	sizzle	wiggle

Synonyms and Antonyms

Write a synonym for each word.

1. center   _____

2. squirm   _____

3. easy   _____

4. stirs   _____

Write an antonym for each word.

5. start   _____

6. sturdy   _____

7. big   _____

8. destroy   _____

Write a word that fits each category.

9. cups, bowls, forks, _____

10. laugh, chuckle, snicker, _____

11. crackle, fizz, hiss, _____

12. hugs, handshakes, high fives, _____

Name: _____ **Date:** _____

Prefixes and Suffixes

Directions: The prefix *mis–* means *wrong*. Add the prefix *mis–* to each word to create a new word.

1. spell _____

2. take _____

3. placed _____

4. behave _____

5. counted _____

6. print _____

7. treat _____

8. matched _____

9. label _____

10. understand _____

Directions: Use a word from your answers above to complete each sentence.

11. I had to add up all my coins again because I _____ the first time.

12. People who _____ their pets should not be allowed to have them.

13. I must have _____ my glasses. I can't find them anywhere!

14. People often _____ big words because they have so many letters.

15. If you make a _____ , just say you're sorry and don't do it again.

16. My sister likes to wear _____ socks on purpose.

Name: _____ **Date:** _____

Directions: Study how the word changes when you add new endings. Add the same endings to each word to create new words.

1. **fix**   fixes   fixing   fixed

   mix   _____   _____   _____

2. **miss**   misses   missing   missed

   kiss   _____   _____   _____

3. **wish**   wishes   wishing   wished

   finish _____   _____   _____

Directions: Find three words in the Word Bank related to each of the spelling words. Write the words on the correct lines.

Word Bank					
simplest	built	builder	dishwasher	giggly	dishes
simply	building	dishcloth	giggles	simplify	giggling

4. build   _____   _____   _____

5. simple   _____   _____   _____

6. giggle   _____   _____   _____

7. dish   _____   _____   _____

Analogies

Name: _____ **Date:** _____

Directions: Use a word from the Word Bank to complete each analogy.

Word Bank					
build	dishes	finish	giggle	griddle	kisses
little	middle	mixes	scribble	sizzle	wiggle

1. **snake** is to **slither** as **worm** is to _____

2. **boiling water** is to **bubble** as **bacon** is to _____

3. **arms** is to **hugs** as **lips** is to _____

4. **hole** is to **dig** as **sandcastle** is to _____

5. **boring** is to **sigh** as **funny** is to _____

6. **knife** is to **cuts** as **spoon** is to _____

7. **enlarge** is to **big** as **shrink** is to _____

8. **A**, **B**, **C**, **D** is to **beginning** as **K**, **L**, **M**, **N** is to _____

9. **neat** is to **print** as **messy** is to _____

10. **first bite** is to **start** as **last bite** is to _____

UNIT 3
Short E Words

Focus

This week's focus is on short *e*, primarily two-syllable words with closed syllables. There is also an emphasis on the *ea* pattern.

Helpful Hint

The vowel team *ea* is a digraph because it makes a single short *e* sound in words such as *head* and *deaf*. When reading an unfamiliar word that contains the *ea* pattern, try the long *e* and short *e* sounds to see which one makes sense.

- ➤ **bread**
- ➤ **breath**
- ➤ **dresses**
- ➤ **health**
- ➤ **heavy**
- ➤ **meddle**
- ➤ **medic**
- ➤ **pebble**
- ➤ **ready**
- ➤ **relish**
- ➤ **selfish**
- ➤ **settle**
- ➤ **spread**
- ➤ **thread**
- ➤ **weather**

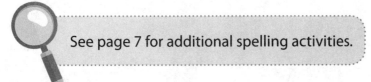

See page 7 for additional spelling activities.

Name: _____ **Date:** _____

Directions: Use a word from the Word Bank to complete each sentence.

Sentence Completions

Word Bank					
breath	dresses	health	heavy	meddle	medic
pebble	ready	relish	spread	thread	weather

1. The _____ is supposed to be rainy all week.

2. That box is too _____ for me to lift on my own.

3. My sister has so many pretty _____ hanging in her closet!

4. I had a hard time catching my _____ after I ran for the bus.

5. In _____ class, we learn how to take care of our bodies.

6. A _____ provided first aid to soldiers who were injured on the battlefield.

7. Are you _____ for school yet? The bus will be here soon!

8. While we were walking on the path, a _____ got stuck in my shoe.

9. Sometimes I put _____ on my hotdog, but usually I just have ketchup.

10. Let's _____ out our towels before we jump in the water.

28631—180 Days of Spelling and Word Study

Name: _____ **Date:**_____

Directions: Use a word from the Word Bank to complete each section.

Word Bank					
bread	dresses	health	heavy	meddle	pebble
ready	relish	selfish	settle	spread	thread

Write a synonym for each word.

1. fitness _____

2. prepared _____

3. interfere _____

4. resolve _____

Write an antonym for each word.

5. light _____

6. boulder _____

7. scrape off _____

8. caring _____

Write a word that fits each category.

9. ketchup, mustard, onions, _____

10. shirts, pants, shoes, _____

11. yarn, ribbon, string, _____

12. bagel, muffin, roll, _____

Sentence Types

Name: _____ **Date:** _____

Directions: Study each example. Write a sentence for each word. End each sentence with the same punctuation as the example.

QUESTION

Ex. *close*:   Did you remember to *close* the door?

1. *ready*: _____

   _____

2. *weather*: _____

   _____

STATEMENT

Ex. *note*:   I wrote a thank you *note* to my friend.

3. *spread*: _____

   _____

4. *health*: _____

   _____

EXCLAMATION

Ex. *bone*:   I found a dinosaur *bone* in my backyard!

5. *breath*: _____

   _____

6. *heavy*: _____

   _____

28631—*180 Days of Spelling and Word Study*   © *Shell Education*

Name: _____ **Date:** _____

Directions: Study how the word changes when you add new endings. Add the same endings to each word to create new words.

1. **dread**   dreads   dreading   dreaded

   thread _____ _____ _____

2. **press**   presses   pressing   pressed

   dress _____ _____ _____

3. **peddle**   peddles   peddling   peddled

   meddle _____ _____ _____

Directions: Find three words in the Word Bank related to each of the spelling words. Write the words on the correct lines.

Word Bank					
settled	heaviest	widespread	bedspread	settlement	breathless
heavier	breathes	spreading	breathing	settler	heavily

4. breath _____ _____ _____

5. settle _____ _____ _____

6. spread _____ _____ _____

7. heavy _____ _____ _____

Name: _____ **Date:** _____

Directions: Use a word from the Word Bank to complete each analogy.

Analogies

Word Bank					
bread	breath	dresses	heavy	medic	pebble
relish	selfish	settle	spread	thread	weather

1. **burrito** is to **tortilla** as **sandwich** is to _____

2. **knit** is to **yarn** as **sew** is to _____

3. **feather** is to **light** as **rock** is to _____

4. **shoes** is to **boots** as **clothes** is to _____

5. **late** is to **time** as **sunny** is to _____

6. **eye** is to **tear** as **lung** is to _____

7. **iceberg** is to **ice cube** as **boulder** is to _____

8. **mystery** is to **solve** as **argument** is to _____

9. **hospital** is to **nurse** as **battlefield** is to _____

10. **share** is to **generous** as **keep** is to _____

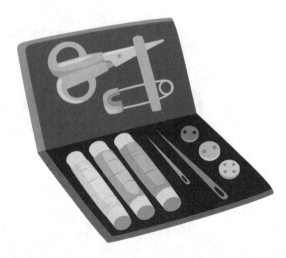

28631—180 Days of Spelling and Word Study   © *Shell Education*

UNIT 4
Short O Words

Focus

This week's focus is on short *o*, primarily two-syllable words with closed syllables.

Helpful Hint

The –*ick* ending only appears at the end of a one-syllable word (*sick*) or at the end of an accented first syllable (*sticker*). When writing two- or three-syllable words that end with /*ik*/, use the –*ic* ending (*topic*, *toxic*).

- ➤ **bottle**
- ➤ **boxes**
- ➤ **comic**
- ➤ **foxes**
- ➤ **gobble**
- ➤ **goggles**
- ➤ **hobble**
- ➤ **nozzle**
- ➤ **optic**
- ➤ **polish**
- ➤ **topic**
- ➤ **topple**
- ➤ **toxic**
- ➤ **tropic**
- ➤ **wobble**

See page 7 for additional spelling activities.

Sentence Completions

Name: _____ **Date:** _____

Directions: Use a word from the Word Bank to complete each sentence.

Word Bank					
bottle	boxes	comic	foxes	gobble	hobble
optic	polish	topic	topple	toxic	tropics

1. If you stack the blocks too high, they will _____ over.

2. Please check to see if we have another _____ of salad dressing in the pantry.

3. I think there's a family of _____ living in my backyard.

4. If you bring cupcakes to the party, the kids will _____ them up.

5. The tank has bright, colorful fish from the _____ .

6. Do you think I should paint my toenails with purple _____ ?

7. My favorite _____ tells jokes about food and video games.

8. I had to _____ all the way home after I twisted my ankle at a neighbor's house.

9. We donated 12 _____ of clothing to the shelter.

10. I still have to choose a _____ for my research project.

Name: _____ **Date:** _____

Directions: Use a word from the Word Bank to complete each section.

Word Bank					
bottle	boxes	comic	foxes	gobble	goggles
hobble	nozzle	polish	topple	toxic	wobble

Synonyms and Antonyms

Write a synonym for each word.

1. comedian _____

2. shine _____

3. limp _____

4. sprayer _____

Write an antonym for each word.

5. healthy _____

6. stand still _____

7. nibble _____

8. build up _____

Write a word that fits each category.

9. jug, jar, can, _____

10. crates, barrels, baskets, _____

11. skunks, squirrels, bears, _____

12. bathing suit, sunscreen, towel, _____

Name: _____ **Date:**_____

Directions: The prefix *non–* means *not*. Add the prefix *non–* to each word to create a new word.

1. fiction _____

2. fat _____

3. stop _____

4. slip _____

5. stick _____

6. violent _____

7. sense _____

8. profit _____

9. refundable _____

10. perishable _____

Directions: Choose a word from your answers above to complete each sentence.

11. I eat _____ yogurt because it has fewer calories.

12. My brother loves reading _____ , but I prefer stories.

13. My _____ socks have rubber grippers on the bottom.

14. What a busy day! We have been going _____ since breakfast.

15. It's easier to cook scrambled eggs in a _____ pan.

16. We brought in _____ foods such as soup and jam for the food drive.

28631—180 Days of Spelling and Word Study

Name: _____ **Date:** _____

Directions: Sort the words in the Word Bank into two categories: *Nouns* and *Verbs*. Write each word in the correct column.

Word Bank				
polished	comic	wobble	goggles	foxes
nozzle	bottle	topple	hobble	gobble

Nouns	Verbs
○	○
○	○
○	○
○	○
○	○

Directions: Write all 10 words in ABC order.

1. _____   6. _____

2. _____   7. _____

3. _____   8. _____

4. _____   9. _____

5. _____   10. _____

Analogies

Name: _____ **Date:**_____

Directions: Use a word from the Word Bank to complete each analogy.

Word Bank					
bottle	boxes	foxes	gobble	goggles	hobble
nozzle	optic	polish	topic	toxic	wobble

1. **tooth** is to **dental** as **eye** is to _____

2. **lips** is to **lipstick** as **nails** is to _____

3. **ears** is to **earplugs** as **eyes** is to _____

4. **eggs** is to **carton** as **ketchup** is to _____

5. **turn on** is to **faucet** as **squeeze** is to _____

6. **slippers** is to **shuffle** as **high heels** is to _____

7. **not hungry** is to **nibble** as **starving** is to _____

8. **medicine** is to **safe** as **poison** is to _____

9. **glass** is to **bottles** as **cardboard** is to _____

10. **chest cold** is to **wheeze** as **sprained ankle** is to _____

UNIT 5
Short U Words

Focus

This week's focus is on short *u*, primarily two-syllable words with closed syllables. There is also an emphasis on the /ŭ/ pattern with *ou* and *o*.

Helpful Hint

The vowel team *ou* sometimes makes a short *u* sound in words such as *double* and *touch*. Words spelled with an *o* can make a short *u* sound when followed by *n* (honey), *v* (love), or *th* (mother).

➤ **bubble**

➤ **country**

➤ **couple**

➤ **cover**

➤ **double**

➤ **front**

➤ **jungle**

➤ **money**

➤ **month**

➤ **public**

➤ **publish**

➤ **punish**

➤ **puzzle**

➤ **touch**

➤ **trouble**

See page 7 for additional spelling activities.

Sentence Completions

Name: _____ Date: _____

Directions: Use a word from the Word Bank to complete each sentence.

Word Bank					
country	couple	cover	double	front	money
month	public	publish	punish	puzzle	touch

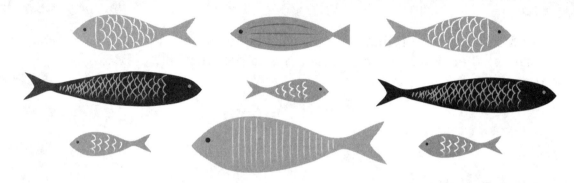

1. Did you hit a _____ or a triple at last night's game?

2. I want to start babysitting so I can earn some _____ .

3. Remember to lock the _____ door when you leave.

4. I finished a jigsaw _____ that had 1,000 pieces!

5. You can't travel to another _____ without a passport.

6. Please don't _____ any of the art projects. They are very fragile.

7. The water will start boiling faster if you _____ the pot.

8. My parents will _____ me if I don't get better grades this term.

9. Next _____ , we're going on a field trip to the aquarium.

10. This is a _____ playground. Anyone's allowed to play here.

Name: _____ **Date:** _____

Directions: Use a word from the Word Bank to complete each section.

Word Bank					
country	couple	cover	double	front	jungle
money	month	public	punish	touch	trouble

Write a synonym for each word.

1. nation _____

2. feel _____

3. pair _____

4. cash _____

Write an antonym for each word.

5. back _____

6. private _____

7. reward _____

8. safety _____

Write a word that fits each category.

9. desert, forest, grassland, _____

10. single, triple, home run, _____

11. week, day, year, _____

12. cap, top, lid, _____

Sentence Types

Name: _____ **Date:**_____

Directions: Study each example. Write a sentence for each word. End each sentence with the same punctuation as the example.

QUESTION

Ex. *close*:   Did you remember to *close* the door?

1. *trouble*: _____

   _____

2. *month*: _____

   _____

STATEMENT

Ex. *note*:   I wrote a thank you *note* to my friend.

3. *front*: _____

   _____

4. *touch*: _____

   _____

EXCLAMATION

Ex. *bone*:   I found a dinosaur *bone* in my backyard!

5. *double*: _____

   _____

6. *money*: _____

   _____

Name: _____ **Date:** _____

Directions: Study how the word changes when you add new endings. Add the same endings to each word to create new words.

1. **hover**   hovers   hovering   hovered

   cover   _____   _____   _____

2. **muzzle**   muzzles   muzzling   muzzled

   puzzle   _____   _____   _____

3. **double**   doubles   doubling   doubled

   trouble   _____   _____   _____

Directions: Find three words in the Word Bank related to each of the spelling words. Write the words on the correct lines.

Word Bank					
bubbly	untouched	published	beachfront	bubblegum	forefront
touches	publication	touching	frontline	publisher	bubbles

4. publish   _____   _____   _____

5. touch   _____   _____   _____

6. front   _____   _____   _____

7. bubble   _____   _____   _____

Analogies

Name: _____ **Date:** _____

Directions: Use a word from the Word Bank to complete each analogy.

Word Bank					
bubble	country	double	front	jungle	money
month	public	publish	punish	puzzle	touch

1. **camel** is to **desert** as **monkey** is to _____

2. **home** is to **private** as **mall** is to _____

3. **Florida** is to **state** as **France** is to _____

4. **splash** is to **puddle** as **pop** is to _____

5. **ingredients** is to **recipe** as **pieces** is to _____

6. **summer** is to **season** as **April** is to _____

7. **nose** is to **smell** as **fingers** is to _____

8. **three times** is to **triple** as **two times** is to _____

9. **backpack** is to **homework** as **wallet** is to _____

10. **albums** is to **release** as **books** is to _____

28631—180 Days of Spelling and Word Study   © *Shell Education*

UNIT 6
ck Pattern

Focus

This week's focus is on *ck* patterns that appear in two-syllable words with closed syllables.

Helpful Hint

The /ĭt/ sound at the end of a two-syllable word is always spelled –*et* when it comes after *ck* (*ticket*, *pocket*).

See page 7 for additional spelling activities.

- bucket
- buckle
- chuckle
- crackle
- freckles
- hockey
- jacket
- jockey
- nickel
- pickle
- pocket
- rocket
- socket
- tackle
- ticket

Name: _____ **Date:** _____

Directions: Use a word from the Word Bank to complete each sentence.

Sentence Completions

Word Bank					
bucket	chuckle	crackle	freckles	hockey	jacket
jockeys	nickels	rockets	socket	tackle	ticket

1. One of the _____ at the Saratoga Races gave me his autograph!

2. In flag football, you're not allowed to _____ your opponent.

3. The _____ on my nose always show up more in the summer.

4. I dumped all the dimes, quarters, and _____ out of my piggy bank.

5. Bring a _____ with you in case it gets chilly on the boat.

6. Put a _____ under the leaky pipe so it doesn't drip onto the floor.

7. Our class built model _____ and launched them behind the school.

8. My friends always _____ when I jump around and act like a monkey.

9. I love listening to the logs _____ while we sit around the campfire.

10. Please plug this cord into the _____ so I can charge my phone.

28631—180 Days of Spelling and Word Study

Name: _____ Date:_____

Directions: The prefix *un–* means *not* or *the opposite of.* Add the prefix *un–* to each word to create a new word.

1. lucky _____

2. steady _____

3. buckle _____

4. zip _____

5. lock _____

6. cover _____

7. wrap _____

8. plug _____

9. helpful _____

10. pack _____

Directions: Choose a word from your answers above to match each description.

11. something you have to do to open your backpack _____

12. something you do when you get home from vacation _____

13. something you do when your phone is done charging _____

14. something you do when your friend gives you a gift _____

15. something you do with a key _____

16. the way most people feel on a balance beam _____

Name: _____ Date:_____

Word Sorts

Directions: Sort the words in the Word Bank into two categories: *Nouns* and *Verbs*. Write each word in the correct column.

Word Bank				
pickle	pocketed	buckled	jockey	tackle
crackle	jacket	nickel	chuckle	bucket

Nouns	Verbs
○	○
○	○
○	○
○	○
○	○

Directions: Write all 10 words in ABC order.

1. _____   6. _____

2. _____   7. _____

3. _____   8. _____

4. _____   9. _____

5. _____   10. _____

  28631—180 Days of Spelling and Word Study

Name: _____ Date:_____

Directions: Study how the word changes when you add new endings. Add the same endings to each word to create new words.

1. **buckle**   buckles   buckling   buckled

   chuckle _____ _____ _____

2. **picket**   pickets   picketing   picketed

   ticket _____ _____ _____

3. **cackle**   cackles   cackling   cackled

   tackle _____ _____ _____

Directions: Find three words in the Word Bank related to each of the spelling words. Write the words on the correct lines.

Word Bank					
crackled	skyrocket	pockets	dill pickle	crackling	rocketed
pocketbook	pickled	pocketful	crackly	pickling	rockets

4. pocket _____ _____ _____

5. crackle _____ _____ _____

6. pickle _____ _____ _____

7. rocket _____ _____ _____

         28631—180 Days of Spelling and Word Study

Inflectional Endings

Name: _____ **Date:** _____

Directions: Use a word from the Word Bank to complete each analogy.

Analogies

Word Bank					
bucket	buckle	chuckle	crackle	hockey	jacket
jockey	nickel	pickle	rocket	socket	ticket

1. **soccer ball** is to **soccer** as **puck** is to _____

2. **race car** is to **driver** as **horse** is to _____

3. **grape** is to **raisin** as **cucumber** is to _____

4. **ten cents** is to **dime** as **five cents** is to _____

5. **coat** is to **zip** as **belt** is to _____

6. **broom** is to **dust pan** as **mop** is to _____

7. **website** is to **password** as **concert** is to _____

8. **bacon** is to **sizzle** as **logs** is to _____

9. **winter** is to **parka** as **spring** is to _____

10. **sob** is to **whimper** as **laugh** is to _____

28631—180 Days of Spelling and Word Study

UNIT 7
Silent Letters

Focus

This week's focus is on silent letters in two-syllable words with closed syllables.

Helpful Hint

Assign, *sign*, *resign*, and *design* all come from the Latin word *signum*, which means *mark* or *sign*. Although the *g* is silent in these words, it is voiced in related words such as *signal*, *signature*, and *designate*.

> assign
> bristle
> bustle
> castle
> climb
> design
> hustle
> knuckle
> nestle
> resign
> rustle
> sign
> whistle
> wrestle
> wriggle

See page 7 for additional spelling activities.

Name: _____ **Date:** _____

Directions: Use a word from the Word Bank to complete each sentence.

Sentence Completions

Word Bank					
assigns	bristles	castle	design	hustle	knuckle
nestle	resign	rustle	sign	whistle	wriggle

1. Ouch! I just scraped my _____ while I was grating the cheese.

2. Mr. Nunes never _____ homework on the weekend.

3. My mom might _____ from her job if she finds a better one.

4. There's a "For Sale" _____ in my neighbor's front yard.

5. This hairbrush has sharp _____ that hurt my scalp.

6. We better _____ or we will be late for the movie!

7. Our dog likes to _____ between my sister and me on the couch.

8. The king's enemies tried to climb over the _____ walls.

9. Someday I'm going to _____ and sew all my own clothes.

10. Our feet _____ in the dry leaves whenever we walk through the woods.

Name: _____ **Date:** _____

Directions: Use a word from the Word Bank to complete each section.

Synonyms and Antonyms

Word Bank					
assign	bristle	castle	climb	design	hustle
knuckle	nestle	resign	whistle	wrestle	wriggle

Write a synonym for each word.

1. palace _____

2. snuggle _____

3. plan _____

4. play rough _____

Write an antonym for each word.

5. hand in _____

6. go down _____

7. move slowly _____

8. accept a job _____

Write a word that fits each category.

9. elbow, ankle, knee, _____

10. twist, wiggle, squirm, _____

11. prickle, whisker, quill, _____

12. blow, pucker, pout, _____

Name: _____ **Date:** _____

Directions: Study each example. Write a sentence for each word. End each sentence with the same punctuation as the example.

QUESTION

Ex. *close*:   Did you remember to *close* the door?

1. *design*: _____

_____

2. *resign*: _____

_____

STATEMENT

Ex. *note*:   I wrote a thank you *note* to my friend.

3. *castle*: _____

_____

4. *bustle*: _____

_____

EXCLAMATION

Ex. *bone*:   I found a dinosaur *bone* in my backyard!

5. *hustle*: _____

_____

6. *wrestle*: _____

_____

Inflectional Endings

Name: _____ **Date:** _____

Directions: Study how the word changes when you add new endings. Add the same endings to each word to create new words.

1. **sign**   signs   signing   signed

   assign _____   _____   _____

2. **hustle**   hustles   hustling   hustled

   bustle _____   _____   _____

3. **nestle**   nestles   nestling   nestled

   wrestle _____   _____   _____

Directions: Find three words in the Word Bank related to each of the spelling words. Write the words on the correct lines.

Word Bank					
climbed	signed	knuckleball	designer	climbing	knucklehead
knuckles	designs	signature	signal	designed	climber

4. design _____   _____   _____

5. climb _____   _____   _____

6. knuckle _____   _____   _____

7. sign _____   _____   _____

Analogies

Name: _____ **Date:** _____

Directions: Use a word from the Word Bank to complete each analogy.

Word Bank					
assign	bristle	castle	climb	design	knuckle
resign	rustle	sign	whistle	wrestle	wriggle

1. **porcupine** is to **quill** as **hairbrush** is to _____

2. **teacher** is to **bell** as **coach** is to _____

3. **president** is to **White House** as **king** is to _____

4. **school** is to **drop out** as **job** is to _____

5. **water** is to **splash** as **dry leaves** is to _____

6. **elevator** is to **ride up** as **ladder** is to _____

7. **arm** is to **elbow** as **finger** is to _____

8. **boxer** is to **box** as **wrestler** is to _____

9. **snake** is to **slither** as **worm** is to _____

10. **purple** is to **color** as **zigzag** is to _____

28631—180 Days of Spelling and Word Study

UNIT 8
Silent E Words

Focus

This week's focus is on silent *e* in two-syllable words as well as silent *e* rule-breakers: *paste, taste, waste*.

Helpful Hint

Most of the words on this list begin with a prefix (*de–, ex–, in–, mis–, pro–, re–*). When breaking the words into syllables, split them after the prefix (*ex·cuse, mis·take, pro·vide*). Also, notice that silent *e* breaks its rule in some words by jumping over two consonants instead of one to make the vowel say its name (*paste, taste, waste*).

See page 7 for additional spelling activities.

- decade
- delete
- excuse
- exhale
- explode
- include
- invite
- mistake
- paste
- promote
- propose
- provide
- refuse
- taste
- waste

Name: _____ **Date:** _____

Directions: Use a word from the Word Bank to complete each sentence.

Word Bank					
decade	delete	excuse	exhales	explode	invite
paste	promote	propose	provide	refuse	waste

1. Firefighters were worried that the building might _____ .

2. If you do a nice job, your boss might _____ you to head chef.

3. Mix the flour and water until it forms a sticky _____ .

4. I can hear Brendan wheeze every time he _____ .

5. Turn off the faucet so you don't _____ water.

6. Please _____ my behavior. I didn't mean to sound rude.

7. We've lived in the same house for more than a _____ .

8. Alex bought a ring and is going to _____ on his date tonight.

9. I _____ to buy you a new hat until you find all the ones you lost!

10. You can _____ all these computer files. I don't need them anymore.

Name: _____   **Date:**_____

Directions: Use a word from the Word Bank to complete each section.

Word Bank					
decade	delete	excuse	exhale	explode	include
mistake	paste	provide	refuse	taste	waste

Synonyms and Antonyms

Write a synonym for each word.

1. error   _____

2. glue   _____

3. burst   _____

4. erase   _____

Write an antonym for each word.

5. inhale   _____

6. exclude   _____

7. conserve   _____

8. say yes   _____

Write a word that fits each category.

9. sight, sound, smell, _____

10. reason, explanation, apology, _____

11. month, year, century, _____

12. protect, promote, propose, _____

Name: _____ **Date:** _____

Directions: The prefix *in–* sometimes means *in*. Add the prefix *in–* to each word or root to create a new word.

1. field _____

2. doors _____

3. mates _____

4. side _____

5. hale _____

6. come _____

7. dent _____

8. ject _____

9. take _____

10. grown _____

Directions: Choose a word from your answers above to complete each sentence.

11. There's a secret pocket _____ my winter coat.

12. My big toe hurts so much because of this _____ toenail.

13. I get a paycheck every week, but I use most of my _____ to pay bills.

14. None of the _____ are allowed to leave the prison.

15. I always _____ deeply before I dive into the pool.

16. Why does the nurse have to _____ me with that sharp needle?

Name: _____ **Date:** _____

Directions: Study how the word changes when you add new endings. Add the same endings to each word to create new words.

1. **inhale**   inhales   inhaling   inhaled

   exhale _____   _____   _____

2. **accuse**   accuses   accusing   accused

   excuse _____   _____   _____

3. **compete**   competes   competing   competed

   delete _____   _____   _____

Directions: Find three words in the Word Bank related to each of the spelling words. Write the words on the correct lines.

Word Bank					
proposal	wasteful	tasteful	explosion	proposing	tasty
taste buds	wasted	exploded	wasting	proposed	explosive

4. taste _____   _____   _____

5. waste _____   _____   _____

6. propose _____   _____   _____

7. explode _____   _____   _____

Name: _____ **Date:** _____

Directions: Use a word from the Word Bank to complete each analogy.

Analogies

Word Bank					
decade	delete	excuse	exhale	explode	include
invite	paste	promote	propose	taste	waste

1. **breathe in** is to **inhale** as **breathe out** is to _____

2. **eyes** is to **see** as **tongue** is to _____

3. **whiteboard** is to **erase** as **computer file** is to _____

4. **court** is to **summon** as **party** is to _____

5. **100 years** is to **century** as **10 years** is to _____

6. **move down** is to **demote** as **move up** is to _____

7. **water pipe** is to **burst** as **gas line** is to _____

8. **refusal** is to **refuse** as **proposal** is to _____

9. **hair** is to **gel** as **tooth** is to _____

10. **leave out** is to **exclude** as **allow in** is to _____

28631—180 Days of Spelling and Word Study

UNIT 9
Soft C Words

Focus

This week's focus is on soft *c* endings in one- and two-syllable words.

Helpful Hint

Hard *c* comes before the vowels *a*, *o*, and *u* as well as the consonants *l* and *r*. Soft *c* only comes before *e*, *i*, and *y*.

➤ chance

➤ dance

➤ decide

➤ device

➤ excite

➤ fancy

➤ fence

➤ glance

➤ once

➤ precise

➤ prince

➤ produce

➤ recite

➤ reduce

➤ since

See page 7 for additional spelling activities.

Name: _____ **Date:** _____

Directions: Use a word from the Word Bank to complete each sentence.

Word Bank					
decide	device	excite	fancy	fence	glance
once	precise	produce	recite	reduce	since

1. Don't even _____ at your phone while you're driving!

2. Keith kicked the ball over the _____ at recess.

3. We haven't had any snow days _____ January.

4. You need to _____ if you're going to grow your hair long or get it cut.

5. Do I have to wear _____ clothes to the party?

6. Do the old mills in upstate New York still _____ paper goods?

7. The kindergartners are now able to _____ the Pledge of Allegiance.

8. I've only been skiing _____ , but I'd like to try it again.

9. It doesn't take much to _____ my little brother. He loves everything!

10. You need to be _____ when you measure the wood or the pieces won't fit.

28631—180 Days of Spelling and Word Study

Name: _____ **Date:** _____

Directions: Use a word from the Word Bank to complete each section.

Word Bank					
chance	dance	device	excite	fancy	fence
glance	once	precise	prince	produce	reduce

Write a synonym for each word.

1. look quickly _____

2. opportunity _____

3. make _____

4. gadget _____

Write an antonym for each word.

5. plain _____

6. vague _____

7. make bigger _____

8. bore _____

Write a word that fits each category.

9. railing, wall, barrier, _____

10. never, twice, always, _____

11. prom, ball, sock hop, _____

12. king, queen, jester, _____

Word Sorts

Name: _____ **Date:**_____

Directions: Sort the words in the Word Bank into two categories: *Soft* c *Words* and *Hard* c *Words*. Then, highlight or circle the letter that comes after *c* in each word, and look for patterns.

Word Bank				
across	because	cattle	classes	compete
couple	cried	cuddle	dance	decide
excuse	fancy	fence	include	once
precise	prince	recite	reduce	since

Soft *c* Words	Hard *c* Words
◯	◯
◯	◯
◯	◯
◯	◯
◯	◯
◯	◯
◯	◯
◯	◯
◯	◯
◯	◯

28631—180 Days of Spelling and Word Study

Name: _____ **Date:** _____

Directions: Study how the word changes when you add new endings. Add the same endings to each word to create new words.

1. prance   prances   prancing   pranced

     glance _____ _____ _____

2. recite   recites   reciting   recited

     excite _____ _____ _____

3. produce   produces   producing   produced

     reduce _____ _____ _____

Directions: Find three words in the Word Bank related to each of the spelling words. Write the words on the correct lines.

Word Bank					
dancer	decided	precisely	productive	danced	deciding
producer	product	decision	dancing	imprecise	precision

4. decide _____ _____ _____

5. dance _____ _____ _____

6. produce _____ _____ _____

7. precise _____ _____ _____

Analogies

Name: _____ **Date:** _____

Directions: Use a word from the Word Bank to complete each analogy.

Word Bank					
dance	decide	device	excite	fancy	fence
glance	once	prince	produce	recite	reduce

1. **two times** is to **twice** as **one time** is to _____

2. **queen** is to **king** as **princess** is to _____

3. **rap** is to **music** as **ballet** is to _____

4. **jeans** is to **casual** as **suit** is to _____

5. **brick** is to **wall** as **chain link** is to _____

6. **dishwasher** is to **appliance** as **tablet** is to _____

7. **store** is to **sell** as **factory** is to _____

8. **song** is to **sing** as **poem** is to _____

9. **boredom** is to **bore** as **excitement** is to _____

10. **collision** is to **collide** as **decision** is to _____

UNIT 10
Soft and Hard G Words

Focus

This week's focus is on soft *g* and hard *g* words.

Helpful Hint

Hard *g* usually comes before the vowels *a, o,* and *u* as well as the consonants *l* and *r*. Soft *g* only comes before *e, i,* and *y*. To keep the *g* hard, add a silent *u* before an *e* (*guest*), *i* (*guilty*), or *y* (*guy*).

- ➤ bridge
- ➤ change
- ➤ cringe
- ➤ gentle
- ➤ guest
- ➤ guide
- ➤ guilty
- ➤ guy
- ➤ judge
- ➤ magic
- ➤ pledge
- ➤ plunge
- ➤ sponge
- ➤ tragic
- ➤ trudge

See page 7 for additional spelling activities.

Name: _____   **Date:** _____

Sentence Completions

Directions: Use a word from the Word Bank to complete each sentence.

Word Bank					
bridge	change	cringe	gentle	guests	guide
guilty	pledge	plunge	sponge	tragic	trudged

1. Please use a _____ to clean up the spill.

2. We always clean our house and put out snacks when _____ come over.

3. She lost her right leg in a _____ car accident.

4. We _____ through the snow in our heavy boots and snow pants.

5. When the water's cold, I just _____ into the deep end.

6. We walked across the _____ and threw pebbles in the water below.

7. A jury will decide if the suspect is _____ or innocent.

8. We had to _____ our plans when we found out it was going to rain.

9. A tour _____ showed us around the museum.

10. In our nature club, we made a _____ to protect animals and their habitats.

Name: _____   **Date:**_____

Directions: Use a word from the Word Bank to complete each section.

Synonyms and Antonyms

Word Bank					
change	cringe	gentle	guest	guide	guilty
judge	magic	pledge	plunge	sponge	trudge

Write a synonym for each word.

1. promise _____

2. dive in _____

3. flinch _____

4. show the way _____

Write an antonym for each word.

5. innocent _____

6. rough _____

7. host _____

8. stay the same _____

Write a word that fits each category.

9. witness, jury, lawyer, _____

10. walk, stroll, limp, _____

11. charms, spells, curses, _____

12. scrub brush, cloth, paper towel, _____

Word Sorts

Name: _____ **Date:** _____

Directions: Sort the words in the Word Bank into two categories: *Soft* g *Words* and *Hard* g *Words*. Then, highlight or circle the letter that comes after *g* in each word, and look for patterns.

Word Bank				
angle	bridge	gather	glossy	gobble
grass	griddle	guess	guest	guide
guilty	gym	judge	magic	pledge
plunge	pudgy	sponge	tragic	trudge

Soft *g* Words	Hard *g* Words
○	○
○	○
○	○
○	○
○	○
○	○
○	○
○	○
○	○
○	○

28631—180 Days of Spelling and Word Study

Name: _____ Date:_____

Directions: Study how the word changes when you add new endings. Add the same endings to each word to create new words.

1. **nudge**   nudges   nudging   nudged

   trudge _____ _____ _____

2. **wedge**   wedges   wedging   wedged

   pledge _____ _____ _____

3. **range**   ranges   ranging   ranged

   change _____ _____ _____

Directions: Find three words in the Word Bank related to each of the spelling words. Write the words on the correct lines.

Word Bank					
guiding	plunging	plunged	spongy	magical	sponging
guidance	sponges	magically	magician	guided	plunger

4. magic _____ _____ _____

5. guide _____ _____ _____

6. sponge _____ _____ _____

7. plunge _____ _____ _____

Name: _____ **Date:** _____

Analogies

Directions: Use a word from the Word Bank to complete each analogy.

Word Bank					
bridge	cringe	guest	guide	guilty	guy
judge	magic	plunge	sponge	tragic	trudge

1. **body** is to **washcloth** as **dishes** is to _____

2. **school** is to **principal** as **courtroom** is to _____

3. **go under** is to **tunnel** as **go over** is to _____

4. **store** is to **customer** as **home** is to _____

5. **woman** is to **lady** as **man** is to _____

6. **cold** is to **shiver** as **embarrassed** is to _____

7. **go high** is to **soar** as **go deep** is to _____

8. **theater** is to **usher** as **museum** is to _____

9. **good** is to **innocent** as **bad** is to _____

10. **talk** is to **drawl** as **walk** is to _____

Unit 11
Consonant Digraphs

Focus

This week's focus is on *gh* and *ph* digraphs and *tch* trigraphs.

Helpful Hint

The *tch* pattern only appears after a short vowel (*catch*, *sketch*, *witch*). Some short vowel words drop the *t* and only use *ch* (*much*, *rich*, *such*).

🔍 See page 7 for additional spelling activities.

WEEK 11

➤ catch

➤ crutches

➤ enough

➤ graphics

➤ laugh

➤ phonics

➤ rough

➤ scratch

➤ sketch

➤ snatch

➤ stitches

➤ stretch

➤ tough

➤ trophy

➤ witch

Name: _____ **Date:** _____

Directions: Use a word from the Word Bank to complete each sentence.

Word Bank					
catch	crutches	enough	laugh	phonics	rough
scratch	snatch	stitches	stretch	tough	trophy

1. I won a _____ for fastest car at the Pinewood Derby.

2. Do I have _____ money left to buy a candy bar?

3. I twisted my ankle so badly that I had to walk on _____ for a week.

4. Don't _____ your bug bites or they'll start to bleed.

5. After sitting at my desk so long, it feels good to stand up and

   _____ .

6. Wash your hands with warm water and soap so you don't

   _____ a cold.

7. Knowing letter sounds, or _____ , helps young children learn to read.

8. It's _____ to finish all my homework on nights that I have soccer.

9. Why did you _____ the remote from your sister?

10. Carter had to get 10 _____ above his eye when he got hit by the baseball.

Name: _____ Date: _____

Directions: Use a word from the Word Bank to complete each section.

Word Bank					
catch	enough	graphics	laugh	rough	scratch
sketch	snatch	stretch	tough	trophy	witch

Write a synonym for each word.

1. grab _____

2. giggle _____

3. scrape _____

4. pictures
on a screen _____

Write an antonym for each word.

5. smooth _____

6. weak _____

7. shrink _____

8. throw _____

Write a word that fits each category.

9. draw, trace, scribble, _____

10. just right, plenty, not too much, _____

11. medal, blue ribbon, prize, _____

12. ghost, princess, cowboy, _____

Name: _____ **Date:** _____

Word Sorts

Directions: Sort the words in the Word Bank into two categories: *Singular Nouns* and *Plural Nouns*. Write each word in the correct column.

Word Bank				
matches	witch	stitches	trophy	crutches
patches	watch	phone	kitchen	photos

Singular Nouns	Plural Nouns
○	○
○	○
○	○
○	○
○	○

Directions: Write all 10 words in ABC order.

1. _____   6. _____

2. _____   7. _____

3. _____   8. _____

4. _____   9. _____

5. _____   10. _____

Name: _____ **Date:** _____

Directions: Study how the word changes when you add new endings. Add the same endings to each word to create new words.

1. **match**   matches   matching   matched

   scratch _____ _____ _____

2. **fetch**   fetches   fetching   fetched

   stretch _____ _____ _____

3. **pitch**   pitches   pitching   pitched

   stitch _____ _____ _____

Directions: Find three words in the Word Bank related to each of the spelling words. Write the words on the correct lines.

Word Bank					
tougher	roughly	laughter	caught	laughing	toughen
laughed	toughest	roughest	rougher	catching	catcher

4. catch _____ _____ _____

5. laugh _____ _____ _____

6. tough _____ _____ _____

7. rough _____ _____ _____

Analogies

Name: _____ **Date:** _____

Directions: Use a word from the Word Bank to complete each analogy.

Word Bank					
catch	crutches	graphics	laugh	phonics	rough
scratch	sketch	stitches	tough	trophy	witch

1. **science** is to **lab** as **reading** is to _____

2. **silk** is to **smooth** as **sandpaper** is to _____

3. **broken bone** is to **cast** as **deep cut** is to _____

4. **swim** is to **pool floats** as **walk** is to _____

5. **howl** is to **werewolf** as **cackle** is to _____

6. **bat** is to **hit** as **mitt** is to _____

7. **contest** is to **prize** as **championship** is to _____

8. **teeth** is to **bite** as **fingernail** is to _____

9. **write** is to **scribble** as **draw** is to _____

10. **book** is to **illustrations** as **online game** is to _____

UNIT 12
Long A Words

Focus

This week's focus is on long *a*, two-syllable words with open syllables.

Helpful Hint

All the words on this list begin with an open syllable (a syllable that ends with a long vowel). When breaking the words into parts, split them after the open syllable. These words are usually divided between a vowel and a consonant (*la·dy, ta·ble, pa·per*).

- able
- baby
- basic
- craters
- crazy
- fable
- gravy
- ladle
- lady
- later
- lazy
- paper
- stable
- staple
- table

See page 7 for additional spelling activities.

Name: _____ **Date:** _____

Directions: Use a word from the Word Bank to complete each sentence.

Sentence Completions

Word Bank					
baby	basic	craters	fable	gravy	ladle
lady	lazy	paper	stable	staple	table

1. My favorite _____ is the story about the lion and the mouse.

2. When you set the _____ , remember to put down forks and knives.

3. Would you like some more _____ on your potatoes?

4. My brother is so _____ , he won't even get off the couch to change the channel.

5. I helped my teacher _____ all the homework packets.

6. When I got lost at the water park, I asked a nice _____ to help me find my mom.

7. Can you add more _____ to the printer? I have three more pages to print.

8. You can use this _____ to scoop stew out of the pot.

9. I'm so excited that my aunt is having a _____ soon. I hope it's a girl!

10. Does each horse have its own stall in the _____ ?

Name: _____ **Date:** _____

Directions: Use a word from the Word Bank to complete each section.

Synonyms and Antonyms

Word Bank					
baby	basic	craters	crazy	fable	gravy
ladle	lady	later	lazy	stable	staple

Write a synonym for each word.

1. infant   _____

2. woman   _____

3. holes   _____

4. big spoon _____

Write an antonym for each word.

5. hardworking _____

6. advanced _____

7. now   _____

8. calm   _____

Write a word that fits each category.

9. glue, rubber band, paper clip, _____

10. barn, hen house, pigsty, _____

11. fairy tale, myth, tall tale, _____

12. sauce, syrup, dressing, _____

Word Sorts

Name: _____ **Date:** _____

Directions: Sort the words in the Word Bank into two categories: *Nouns* and *Adjectives*. Write each word in the correct column.

Word Bank				
crazy	gravy	lady	lazy	basic
paper	able	hazy	baby	table

Nouns	Adjectives
○	○
○	○
○	○
○	○
○	○

Directions: Write all 10 words in ABC order.

1. _____
2. _____
3. _____
4. _____
5. _____

6. _____
7. _____
8. _____
9. _____
10. _____

Name: _____ **Date:**_____

Directions: Answer each question in a complete sentence. Turn the question around, and use the bold word in your answer.

1. Why do people read **fables**?

_____

_____

2. What do you like to do at your kitchen **table**?

_____

_____

3. What are three reasons why a **baby** might cry?

_____

_____

4. Why do people use a **ladle** to scoop soups and stews?

_____

_____

5. Where does **paper** come from?

_____

_____

Name: _____ **Date:**_____

Directions: Use a word from the Word Bank to complete each analogy.

Word Bank					
baby	basic	craters	fable	gravy	ladle
lady	later	lazy	paper	stable	table

1. **french fries** is to **ketchup** as **mashed potatoes** is to _____

2. **do homework** is to **desk** as **eat dinner** is to _____

3. **man** is to **gentleman** as **woman** is to _____

4. **litter box** is to **cat** as **diaper** is to _____

5. **Cinderella** is to **fairy tale** as **tortoise and hare** is to _____

6. **hen** is to **chicken coop** as **horse** is to _____

7. **ice cream** is to **scoop** as **soup** is to _____

8. **painting** is to **canvas** as **drawing** is to _____

9. **563 x 274** is to **advanced** as **2 + 2** is to _____

10. **yesterday** is to **earlier** as **tomorrow** is to _____

Analogies

UNIT 13
Long A Vowel Teams

Focus

This week's focus is on long *a* vowel teams in two-syllable words. Also, two new long *a* patterns are introduced: *ei* and *eigh*.

Helpful Hint

The most common long *a* vowel teams are *ai* and *ay*. Use *ai* at the beginning of a word or in the middle of a word (*air*, *stain*) and *ay* at the end of a syllable or word (*cray·on*, *play*).

- afraid
- betray
- delay
- details
- eight
- exclaim
- explain
- freight
- holiday
- praise
- raise
- sleigh
- veil
- veins
- weigh

See page 7 for additional spelling activities.

Name: _____ **Date:** _____

Directions: Use a word from the Word Bank to complete each sentence.

Word Bank					
afraid	betray	delay	details	exclaim	explain
freight	holiday	praise	sleighs	veil	veins

Sentence Completions

1. The truck driver unloaded his _____ from the back of the truck.

2. I don't understand this game. Can you _____ the rules to me?

3. I could hear him _____ "Bingo!" from across the room.

4. We had a two hour _____ this morning for our flight.

5. I added _____ to my story to make it more interesting.

6. Why do the _____ in my wrist look blue?

7. I used to be _____ of the dark, but not anymore!

8. Long ago, horses pulled _____ through the snow.

9. Is your aunt going to wear a _____ with her wedding gown?

10. Victor is very loyal and would never _____ his friends.

Name: _____ Date: _____

Directions: The prefix *ex–* sometimes means *out*. Add the prefix *ex–* to each word or root to create a real word.

1. clude _____

2. it _____

3. port _____

4. plain _____

5. claim _____

6. pire _____

7. tinct _____

8. pel _____

9. hale _____

10. tend _____

Directions: Choose a word from your answers above to match each description.

11. breathe **out** _____

12. leave a person **out** _____

13. shout **out** suddenly and loudly _____

14. stretch **out** _____

15. the way **out** of a room or building _____

16. kick a student **out** of school _____

Name: _____ **Date:** _____

Directions: Sort the words in the Word Bank into two categories: *Nouns* and *Verbs*. Write each word in the correct column.

Word Bank				
exclaim	explain	sleigh	crayons	veil
weigh	veins	delay	raise	freight

Nouns	Verbs
○	○
○	○
○	○
○	○
○	○

Directions: Write all 10 words in ABC order.

1. _____   6. _____

2. _____   7. _____

3. _____   8. _____

4. _____   9. _____

5. _____   10. _____

Name: _____ **Date:**_____

Directions: Answer each question in a complete sentence. Turn the question around, and use the bold word in your answer.

1. Why do doctors have to **weigh** children during their checkups?

   _____

   _____

2. Why do people **exclaim** loudly when they stub their toes?

   _____

   _____

3. What do you like to do on your favorite **holiday**?

   _____

   _____

4. Why are some children **afraid** of the dark?

   _____

   _____

5. Why do you need to **raise** your hand in class?

   _____

   _____

Turn the Question Around

Name: _____ Date:_____

Directions: Use a word from the Word Bank to complete each analogy.

Word Bank					
afraid	delay	eight	exclaim	freight	holiday
praise	raise	sleigh	veil	veins	weigh

1. **summer** is to **season** as **Halloween** is to _____

2. **queen** is to **crown** as **bride** is to _____

3. **insect** is to **six** as **spider** is to _____

4. **ship** is to **cargo** as **train** is to _____

5. **put down** is to **lower** as **lift up** is to _____

6. **air** is to **lungs** as **blood** is to _____

7. **ruler** is to **measure** as **scale** is to _____

8. **insult** is to **criticize** as **compliment** is to _____

9. **softly** is to **whisper** as **loudly** is to _____

10. **horses** is to **wagon** as **reindeer** is to _____

UNIT 14
Long E Vowel Teams

➤ **breathe**
➤ **breeze**
➤ **cheese**
➤ **crease**
➤ **freeze**
➤ **grease**
➤ **lease**
➤ **leave**
➤ **peace**
➤ **please**
➤ **sleeve**
➤ **sneeze**
➤ **squeeze**
➤ **weave**
➤ **wheeze**

Focus

This week's focus is on long *e* vowel teams in one-syllable words that end with silent *e*.

Helpful Hint

The silent *e* at the end of these words is not needed to make the vowels long, since they all contain a vowel team. In some cases, the silent *e* makes the *c* sound like /s/ and the *s* sound like /z/. In words that end with –*ve* or –*ze*, the *e* is just there for company since no English words end with –*v*, and very few words end with –*z*.

See page 7 for additional spelling activities.

Sentence Completions

Name: _____ **Date:** _____

Directions: Use a word from the Word Bank to complete each sentence.

Word Bank					
breathe	breeze	cheese	creases	freeze	grease
lease	leave	peace	sleeve	sneeze	squeeze

1. I can't _____ any more toothpaste out of the tube.

2. My asthma makes it hard for me to _____ sometimes.

3. I ordered extra _____ on our pizza.

4. Use hot water and soap to wash the _____ off the frying pan.

5. I hope the two countries stop fighting and reach a _____ agreement.

6. I filled up the ice cube trays and waited for the water to _____ .

7. I folded my paper twice and made sharp _____ .

8. Did your uncle sign a _____ for his new apartment yet?

9. Remember to cover your mouth when you _____ .

10. It is rude to _____ in the middle of a band or chorus concert.

Name: _____ **Date:** _____

Directions: Use a word from the Word Bank to complete each section.

Word Bank					
breathe	breeze	cheese	crease	freeze	grease
leave	peace	please	sneeze	squeeze	weave

Write a synonym for each word.

1. inhale and exhale _____

2. oil   _____

3. press together _____

4. mild wind _____

Write an antonym for each word.

5. war   _____

6. melt   _____

7. come   _____

8. unravel   _____

Write a word that fits each category.

9. lettuce, pickles, ketchup, _____

10. yawn, cough, burp, _____

11. excuse me, thank you, I'm sorry, _____

12. fold, pleat, wrinkle, _____

Name: _____   **Date:** _____

Directions: Study how the word changes when you add new endings. Add the same endings to each word to create new words.

1. **wheeze**   wheezes   wheezing   wheezed

   squeeze _____   _____   _____

   sneeze _____   _____   _____

2. **sheathe**   sheathes   sheathing   sheathed

   breathe _____   _____   _____

Directions: Find three words in the Word Bank related to each of the spelling words. Write the words on the correct lines.

Word Bank					
cheeseburger	frozen	pleasing	cheesecake	leaving	pleasure
freezing	cheesy	freezer	left	leaves	pleasant

3. freeze   _____   _____   _____

4. leave   _____   _____   _____

5. cheese   _____   _____   _____

6. please   _____   _____   _____

Name: _____ **Date:** _____

Directions: Answer each question in a complete sentence. Turn the question around, and use the bold word in your answer.

1. What kind of medicine can people use when they start to **wheeze**?

   _____

   _____

2. Why is it important to say "**please**" and "thank you"?

   _____

   _____

3. Why does a boa constrictor **squeeze** its prey?

   _____

   _____

4. Why do you need to **grease** the pan when you bake a cake?

   _____

   _____

5. What are some foods that contain **cheese**?

   _____

   _____

Turn the Question Around

© Shell Education

Name: _____ **Date:** _____

Directions: Use a word from the Word Bank to complete each analogy.

Analogies

Word Bank					
breathe	breeze	cheese	crease	freeze	lease
leave	sleeve	sneeze	squeeze	weave	wheeze

1. **foot** is to **shoe** as **arm** is to _____

2. **sweater** is to **knit** as **basket** is to _____

3. **rainstorm** is to **sprinkle** as **wind** is to _____

4. **oven** is to **cook** as **freezer** is to _____

5. **brain** is to **think** as **lungs** is to _____

6. **sundae** is to **sprinkles** as **pizza** is to _____

7. **cough drop** is to **cough** as **inhaler** is to _____

8. **sleepiness** is to **yawn** as **allergies** is to _____

9. **buy** is to **deed** as **rent** is to _____

10. **entrance** is to **come in** as **exit** is to _____

UNIT 15
More Long E Vowel Teams

Focus

This week's focus is on long *e* vowel teams in two-syllable words. Two new long *e* patterns are introduced: *ei* and *eo*.

Helpful Hint

The letter *a* often makes a schwa sound /ə/ at the beginning of a word. When breaking these words into syllables, divide after the *a* (*a·sleep*, *a·gree*).

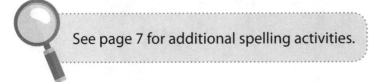

See page 7 for additional spelling activities.

- agree
- asleep
- beetle
- beneath
- between
- ceiling
- deceive
- eagle
- easy
- either
- needle
- people
- receive
- steeple
- weird

Name: _____ **Date:** _____

Directions: Use a word from the Word Bank to complete each sentence.

Word Bank					
agree	asleep	beneath	ceiling	deceive	eagle
easy	either	needle	people	receive	steeple

1. A lot of _____ like to start their holiday shopping on Black Friday.

2. Look up! There's a giant spider crawling on the _____ .

3. Riding a bike is _____ once you learn how to do it.

4. Did you _____ any birthday cards in the mail?

5. The bald _____ was chosen as our national bird in 1782.

6. From across town, we could hear the church bells ringing from the tall

   _____ .

7. Make sure you know what you're buying. Don't let flashy ads

   _____ you.

8. I keep some of my toys in storage bins _____ my bed.

9. Do you _____ that we should not get homework on the weekend?

10. I pretended I was _____ when Mom came in to check on me.

Name: _____ **Date:** _____

Directions: Use a word from the Word Bank to complete each section.

Word Bank					
asleep	beetle	between	ceiling	deceive	eagle
easy	needle	people	receive	steeple	weird

Write a synonym for each word.

1. humans _____

2. strange _____

3. church tower _____

4. trick _____

Write an antonym for each word.

5. give _____

6. difficult _____

7. awake _____

8. floor _____

Write a word that fits each category.

9. hawk, falcon, seagull, _____

10. ladybug, ant, cockroach, _____

11. over, under, around, _____

12. thread, pins, fabric, _____

Name: _____ **Date:** _____

Directions: The suffix *–ful* means *full of.* The suffix *–less* means *without.* Add *–ful* or *–less* to each underlined word to create a real word.

1. without <u>fear</u> _____

2. full of <u>cheer</u> _____

3. without <u>sleeves</u> _____

4. full of <u>tears</u> _____

5. without <u>sleep</u> _____

6. without <u>speech</u> _____

7. full of <u>peace</u> _____

8. without <u>use</u> _____

9. full of <u>grace</u> _____

10. full of <u>care</u> _____

Directions: Choose a word from your answers above to match each description.

11. a shirt that shows your arms _____

12. the view from the dock of a quiet lake _____

13. a sad goodbye when your best friend moves away _____

14. the way you feel when you're too shocked to talk _____

15. a ballerina who can balance on her tiptoes _____

16. an old clock that doesn't work anymore _____

Name: _____ **Date:** _____

Directions: Answer each question in a complete sentence. Turn the question around, and use the bold word in your answer.

1. Why do children put teeth **beneath** their pillows?

   _____

   _____

2. Why are some people afraid of **needles**?

   _____

   _____

3. Why is it important for **people** to wash their hands often?

   _____

   _____

4. Which school subjects are **easy** for you?

   _____

   _____

5. How do cobwebs get on the **ceiling**?

   _____

   _____

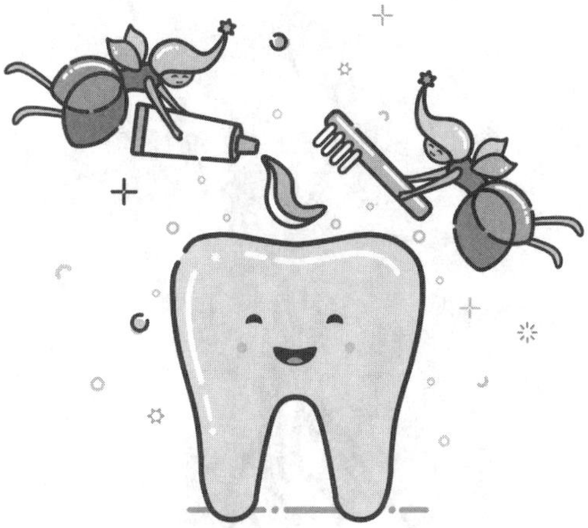

Analogies

Name: _____ **Date:** _____

Directions: Use a word from the Word Bank to complete each analogy.

Word Bank					
agree	asleep	beetle	between	ceiling	eagle
easy	either	needle	people	receive	steeple

1. **cut** is to **knife** as **sew** is to _____

2. **no** is to **disagree** as **yes** is to _____

3. **day** is to **awake** as **night** is to _____

4. **child** is to **children** as **person** is to _____

5. **below** is to **floor** as **above** is to _____

6. **national tree** is to **oak** as **national bird** is to _____

7. **nor** is to **neither** as **or** is to _____

8. **"You're welcome"** is to **give** as **"Thank you"** is to _____

9. **hop** is to **cricket** as **crawl** is to _____

10. **frosting** is to **on top** as **cream filling** is to _____

UNIT 16
Long *I* Vowel Team and Open Syllables

Focus

This week's focus is on long *i*, two-syllable words with open syllables. A new long *i* vowel team is introduced: *ia*.

Helpful Hint

Y makes a long *e* sound at the end of a word when it follows a consonant in an unaccented syllable (*fun·ny*, *ba·by*). *Y* makes a long *i* sound at the end of a word when it follows a consonant in an accented syllable (*re·ply*, *de·ny*).

➤ apply
➤ buy
➤ deny
➤ dial
➤ icy
➤ July
➤ lightning
➤ rely
➤ reply
➤ slimy
➤ spider
➤ supply
➤ tiger
➤ title
➤ trial

See page 7 for additional spelling activities.

Name: _____ **Date:** _____

Directions: Use a word from the Word Bank to complete each sentence.

Word Bank					
apply	buy	deny	dial	icy	lightning
rely	reply	spider	tiger	title	trial

Sentence Completions

1. Watch out for _____ if you go camping during a thunderstorm.

2. Are you going to _____ for a job at the ice cream shop?

3. A big, creepy _____ crawled across my sleeping bag.

4. What was the _____ of that movie we watched last weekend?

5. Dad's taking me to _____ new cleats and a mouth guard tomorrow.

6. I know you ate all the cookies. Don't even try to _____ it!

7. My favorite animal at the zoo was a 600-pound _____ from China.

8. Did you _____ to Grandma's email yet?

9. Remember to _____ 911 if there's an emergency.

10. The criminal _____ lasted three weeks and was all over the news.

Name: _____ **Date:** _____

Directions: Use a word from the Word Bank to complete each section.

Word Bank					
buy	deny	dial	icy	July	rely
reply	slimy	supply	tiger	title	trial

Write a synonym for each word.

1. answer _____

2. cold _____

3. purchase _____

4. depend on _____

Write an antonym for each word.

5. admit _____

6. hang up _____

7. dry _____

8. demand _____

Write a word that fits each category.

9. February, March, October, _____

10. judge, courtroom, verdict, _____

11. author's name, illustrator's name, picture, _____

12. lion, cheetah, jaguar, _____

Name: _____ **Date:** _____

Directions: Study how the word changes when you add new endings. Add the same endings to each word to create new words.

1. **apply**   applies   applying   applied

   supply   _____   _____   _____

2. **cry**   cries   crying   cried

   rely   _____   _____   _____

3. **brighten**   brightens   brightening   brightened

   frighten _____   _____   _____

Directions: Find three words in the Word Bank related to each of the spelling words. Write the words on the correct lines.

Word Bank					
icing	lighten	buying	denied	bought	iced
buys	lightness	denial	ice rink	denying	light

4. buy   _____   _____   _____

5. deny   _____   _____   _____

6. icy   _____   _____   _____

7. lightning _____   _____   _____

Name: _____ Date:_____

Directions: The suffix *-ness* means *a state of being.* Adding *-ness* to the end of a word changes it from an adjective to a noun. Add *-ness* to the end of each adjective.

1. shy _____

2. tight _____

3. dry _____

4. blind _____

5. kind _____

6. ill _____

7. fresh _____

8. weak _____

9. dark _____

10. thick _____

Directions: Choose a word from your answers above to match each description.

11. the reason people need a flashlight at night _____

12. a reason someone might need a guide dog _____

13. a reason kids have to stay home from school _____

14. a reason kids might not make eye contact or talk a lot _____

15. a reason people might ask for a sip of water _____

16. something that makes people feel happy and loved _____

Analogies

Name: _____ **Date:** _____

Directions: Use a word from the Word Bank to complete each analogy.

Word Bank					
apply	buy	deny	dial	July	lightning
rely	slimy	spider	tiger	title	trial

1. **wild dog** is to **wolf** as **wild cat** is to _____

2. **Dr. Seuss** is to **author** as *Green Eggs and Ham* is to _____

3. **library** is to **borrow** as **bookstore** is to _____

4. **boom** is to **thunder** as **flash** is to _____

5. **six legs** is to **insect** as **eight legs** is to _____

6. **chick** is to **fuzzy** as **worm** is to _____

7. **"I did it"** is to **admit** as **"I didn't do it"** is to _____

8. **dependable** is to **depend** as **reliable** is to _____

9. **auction items** is to **bid** as **job openings** is to _____

10. **email address** is to **type** as **phone number** is to _____

UNIT 17
Long O Vowel Team

Focus

This week's focus is on two-syllable words with *ow*.

Helpful Hint

The most common long *o* vowel teams are *oa* and *ow*. The *oa* pattern always appears at the beginning or in the middle of a word (*oats*, *throat*). The *ow* vowel team usually appears at the end of a word or syllable (*be·low*, *bow·tie*). Adding *n* to the end of a word that ends with *ow* shows its past participle.

- below
- bowl
- elbow
- follow
- grown
- hollow
- meadow
- mellow
- pillow
- rainbow
- shadow
- shallow
- widow
- window
- yellow

See page 7 for additional spelling activities.

Name: _____ Date:_____

Sentence Completions

Directions: Use a word from the Word Bank to complete each sentence.

Word Bank					
bowl	follow	grown	hollow	meadow	mellow
pillow	shadow	shallow	widow	window	yellow

1. May I have a _____ of cereal?

2. After I lost my tooth, I put it under my _____ .

3. Let's open the _____ so we can get some fresh air.

4. Some owls make their nests inside _____ tree trunks.

5. My puppy likes to _____ me around the house.

6. Adeline wore a bright _____ dress to the Easter egg hunt.

7. We saw 12 butterflies when we walked to the _____ to pick wildflowers.

8. My cousin Eddie is _____ , but his little brother is wild!

9. I can't believe how much you've _____ since the last time I saw you!

10. I have to stay in the _____ end of the pool unless my parents swim with me.

Name: _____ **Date:** _____

Directions: Use a word from the Word Bank to complete each section.

Synonyms and Antonyms

Word Bank					
below	bowl	elbow	follow	hollow	meadow
mellow	pillow	shadow	shallow	widow	yellow

Write a synonym for each word.

1. field _____

2. shade _____

3. under _____

4. cushion _____

Write an antonym for each word.

5. solid _____

6. lead _____

7. hyper _____

8. deep _____

Write a word that fits each category.

9. ankle, knee, wrist, _____

10. purple, green, orange, _____

11. dish, cup, platter, _____

12. wife, fiancée, girlfriend, _____

Word Sorts

Name: _____ **Date:** _____

Directions: Sort the words in the Word Bank into two categories: *Adjectives* and *Nouns.* Write each word in the correct column.

Word Bank				
yellow	pillow	window	hollow	mellow
widow	shallow	bowl	meadow	narrow

Adjectives	Nouns
○	○
○	○
○	○
○	○
○	○

Directions: Write all 10 words in ABC order.

1. _____   6. _____

2. _____   7. _____

3. _____   8. _____

4. _____   9. _____

5. _____   10. _____

28631—180 Days of Spelling and Word Study

Name: _____ **Date:** _____

Directions: Answer each question in a complete sentence. Turn the question around, and use the bold word in your answer.

1. Why should young children stay in the **shallow** end of a pool?

    _____

    _____

2. Why do ducklings **follow** their mother?

    _____

    _____

3. Why are **shadows** shorter in the middle of the day?

    _____

    _____

4. Why do people wear **elbow** pads when they're skateboarding or rollerblading?

    _____

    _____

5. What are some foods that are **yellow**?

    _____

    _____

Name: _____ **Date:** _____

Directions: Use a word from the Word Bank to complete each analogy.

Analogies

Word Bank					
below	bowl	elbow	grown	hollow	meadow
pillow	rainbow	shallow	widow	window	yellow

1. **cake** is to **plate** as **ice cream** is to _____

2. **leg** is to **knee** as **arm** is to _____

3. **wood** is to **door** as **glass** is to _____

4. **grass** is to **green** as **sun** is to _____

5. **couch** is to **cushion** as **bed** is to _____

6. **dark** is to **shadow** as **colorful** is to _____

7. **water lilies** is to **pond** as **wildflowers** is to _____

8. **dive** is to **deep** as **wade** is to _____

9. **look up** is to **above** as **look down** is to _____

10. **know** is to **known** as **grow** is to _____

28631—180 Days of Spelling and Word Study

UNIT 18
Long O Patterns

Focus

This week's focus is on long *o*, primarily two-syllable words with open syllables.

Helpful Hint

Sometimes nouns can be changed to adjectives by adding a –*y* at the end. If a noun ends with *e*, remember to drop the *e* before adding the –*y* (*bone/bony, smoke/smoky*).

- bony
- boulder
- dough
- ghost
- hotel
- noble
- poll
- program
- robot
- scroll
- shoulder
- smoky
- stroll
- though
- toll

See page 7 for additional spelling activities.

Sentence Completions

Name: _____ **Date:** _____

Directions: Use a word from the Word Bank to complete each sentence.

Word Bank					
dough	ghost	hotel	noble	poll	program
robot	scroll	shoulder	smoky	though	toll

1. I always record my favorite _____ so I can watch it later.

2. Even _____ I twisted my ankle, I still want to play in the soccer game.

3. You need to roll out the cookie _____ first and then use the cookie cutters.

4. Let's check in to our _____ room first before we start exploring the city.

5. The air was so _____ that I had to move to the other side of the campfire.

6. A butterfly swooped down and landed right on my _____ .

7. We turned this old white sheet into a cute _____ costume.

8. You have to pay a _____ when you get off the highway.

9. Our teacher took a _____ to see what we'd like to do on field day.

10. If you _____ down, you'll see a button that brings you to online games.

28631—180 Days of Spelling and Word Study

Name: _____   **Date:** _____

Directions: Use a word from the Word Bank to complete each section.

Word Bank					
bony	boulder	dough	ghost	hotel	noble
poll	program	shoulder	smoky	stroll	toll

Write a synonym for each word.

1. survey   _____

2. fee   _____

3. honorable   _____

4. show   _____

Write an antonym for each word.

5. plump   _____

6. clear   _____

7. walk quickly   _____

8. pebble   _____

Write a word that fits each category.

9. motel, inn, bed and breakfast, _____

10. ankle, knee, waist, _____

11. witch, skeleton, mummy, _____

12. batter, mixture, blend, _____

Homophones

Name: _____ **Date:** _____

Directions: Homophones sound the same but have different spellings and meanings. Write the correct homophone on each line.

1. Sometimes firefighters slide down a _____ instead of using the stairs.
   (pole/poll)

2. I had a buttered _____ with my dinner.
   (role/roll)

3. We saw a _____ and her baby standing behind those trees!
   (doe/dough)

4. Please _____ the door. You're letting all the cold air in.
   (close/clothes)

5. I can't believe how much you've _____ since last year!
   (groan/grown)

6. Who is playing the _____ of Snow White in your school play?
   (role/roll)

7. Have you _____ Dad your report card yet?
   (shone/shown)

8. I poured extra chocolate chips into the cookie _____ .
   (doe/dough)

9. Why do you _____ every time you do a sit-up?
   (groan/grown)

10. The sun _____ so brightly, I needed sunglasses.
    (shone/shown)

Name: _____ **Date:** _____

Directions: Study how the word changes when you add new endings. Add the same endings to each word to create new words.

1. **roll**   rolls   rolling   rolled

   poll   _____   _____   _____

2. **hollow**   hollows   hollowing   hollowed

   follow _____   _____   _____

3. **toast**   toasts   toasting   toasted

   boast   _____   _____   _____

Directions: Find three words in the Word Bank related to each of the spelling words. Write the words on the correct lines.

Word Bank					
stroller	doughy	smoke	bone	doughnut	bone-chilling
backbone	smoking	smokehouse	doughboy	strolled	strolling

4. smoky _____   _____   _____

5. bony _____   _____   _____

6. stroll _____   _____   _____

7. dough _____   _____   _____

Name: _____ **Date:**_____

Directions: Use a word from the Word Bank to complete each analogy.

Word Bank					
boulder	dough	hotel	poll	program	robot
scroll	shoulders	smoky	stroll	though	toll

1. **pancake** is to **batter** as **cookie** is to _____

2. **nod** is to **head** as **shrug** is to _____

3. **born** is to **person** as **built** is to _____

4. **talk** is to **chat** as **walk** is to _____

5. **eat** is to **restaurant** as **sleep** is to _____

6. **stream** is to **river** as **pebble** is to _____

7. **make** is to **produce** as **TV show** is to _____

8. **boiling water** is to **steamy** as **fire** is to _____

9. **subway** is to **fare** as **highway** is to _____

10. **pen** is to **paper** as **quill and ink** is to _____

UNIT 19
Long U Patterns

Focus

This week's focus is on long *u* patterns in one-syllable words. Two new long *u* patterns are introduced: *ou* and *o*-consonant-*e*. The *ui* pattern in these words makes the /*oo*/ sound.

Helpful Hint

Many people confuse the spellings of *loose* and *lose*. If you're confused, remember this trick: The word *lose* loses an *o*! Also, silent *e* has many jobs on this list. It makes *s* sound like /*z*/ and *c* sound like /*s*/. It also keeps *v* company at the end of a word.

See page 7 for additional spelling activities.

- bruise
- choose
- cruel
- cruise
- fuel
- group
- juice
- loose
- lose
- move
- prove
- route
- soup
- through
- truth

Name: _____ **Date:** _____

Directions: Use a word from the Word Bank to complete each sentence.

Word Bank					
bruise	choose	cruise	juice	loose	lose
move	prove	route	soup	through	truth

1. We had to take an alternate _____ because of roadwork.

2. My parents went on an ocean _____ for their anniversary.

3. We walked _____ a huge crowd of people on the sidewalk.

4. You can _____ French fries or rice for your side dish.

5. I keep wiggling my _____ tooth, but it won't come out.

6. You should always tell your parents the _____ , even if you get in trouble.

7. Would you like a glass of orange _____ with your breakfast?

8. My family might _____ to Hong Kong if my dad gets transferred there.

9. Nothing warms you up like a bowl of _____ and a mug of hot chocolate.

10. Let's write your name inside your jacket in case you _____ it.

Name: _____ Date: _____

Directions: Use a word from the Word Bank to complete each section.

Word Bank					
bruise	choose	cruel	cruise	fuel	juice
loose	lose	move	soup	through	truth

Write a synonym for each word.

1. boat ride _____

2. gasoline _____

3. select _____

4. evil _____

Write an antonym for each word.

5. tight _____

6. lies _____

7. find _____

8. stay still _____

Write a word that fits each category.

9. scrape, blister, cut, _____

10. stew, chowder, broth, _____

11. over, under, around, _____

12. eggs, toast, coffee, _____

Synonyms and Antonyms

Homophones

Name: _____ **Date:** _____

Directions: Homophones sound the same but have different spellings and meanings. Write the correct homophone on each line.

1. When Dad _____ the ball to me, it bounced out of my mitt.
   (through/threw)

2. My brother always _____ with his mouth open. Yuck!
   (chews/choose)

3. When you pull weeds, remember to grab their _____ too.
   (roots/routes)

4. I ate _____ many sweets, so now I have a bellyache.
   (to/too/two)

5. Which toy did you _____ from the prize box?
   (chews/choose)

6. You have to walk _____ the kitchen to get to the dining room.
   (through/threw)

7. Can I come with you _____ the store?
   (to/too/two)

8. The weather was windy, so we _____ our kites on the beach.
   (flew/flu)

9. Do you have _____ sisters or three?
   (to/too/two)

10. When my cousin caught the _____ , she missed a week of school.
    (flew/flu)

Name: _____ **Date:** _____

Directions: Answer each question in a complete sentence. Turn the question around, and use the bold word in your answer.

1. Why does **soup** make a good meal on a cold evening?

   _____

   _____

2. Why do some teachers assign **group** projects?

   _____

   _____

3. Why is it important to be a good sport when you **lose** a game?

   _____

   _____

4. Why is it a good idea to **choose** the clothes you will wear to school at night?

   _____

   _____

5. What are three types of **juice**?

   _____

   _____

Analogies

Name: _____ **Date:** _____

Directions: Use a word from the Word Bank to complete each analogy.

Word Bank					
bruise	choose	cruel	cruise	fuel	group
prove	loose	lose	move	soup	through

1. **fork** is to **noodles** as **spoon** is to _____

2. **plane** is to **flight** as **ship** is to _____

3. **guess** is to **question** as **solve** is to _____

4. **victory** is to **win** as **loss** is to _____

5. **too small** is to **tight** as **too big** is to _____

6. **one** is to **individual** as **several** is to _____

7. **apple** is to **food** as **gasoline** is to _____

8. **bridge** is to **over** as **tunnel** is to _____

9. **card game** is to **flip** as **chess game** is to _____

10. **friend** is to **kind** as **bully** is to _____

UNIT 20
More Long U Patterns

Focus

This week's focus is on long *u* vowel teams in two-syllable words and long *u* patterns at the end of an open syllable.

Helpful Hint

When dividing words into syllables, remember that every syllable needs to have at least one vowel in it (*noo·dle, du·ty*). In some cases, *y* is used as a vowel. Syllables do not have to contain a consonant (*val·ue, u·nit*).

- argue
- balloon
- bugle
- cartoon
- duty
- improve
- music
- nephew
- noodle
- pursue
- recruit
- remove
- rescue
- shampoo
- value

See page 7 for additional spelling activities.

Name: _____ **Date:** _____

Directions: Use a word from the Word Bank to complete each sentence.

Sentence Completions

Word Bank					
argue	balloon	cartoons	duty	improve	music
pursue	recruit	remove	rescue	shampoo	value

1. I tied the _____ around my wrist so it wouldn't float away.

2. What kind of _____ do you like to listen to?

3. We're trying to _____ more players for our flag football team.

4. You'll get more _____ for your money if you buy the larger boxes of cereal.

5. Make sure you rinse out all the _____ or your hair will look greasy.

6. I like to watch _____ on Saturday mornings.

7. Don't _____ the tags from those clothes until you make sure they fit.

8. I hate when my friends _____ over what to do at recess.

9. Lifeguards are trained to _____ people who are drowning.

10. A nurse's _____ is to take care of his or her patients.

Name: _____ **Date:** _____

Directions: Use a word from the Word Bank to complete each section.

Word Bank					
balloons	bugle	duty	improve	music	nephew
pursue	recruit	remove	rescue	shampoo	value

Write a synonym for each word.

1. worth _____

2. save _____

3. chase _____

4. responsibility _____

Write an antonym for each word.

5. put in _____

6. get worse _____

7. niece _____

8. turn away _____

Write a word that fits each category.

9. streamers, confetti, centerpiece, _____

10. gym, art, library, _____

11. soap, body wash, conditioner, _____

12. trumpet, sax, flute, _____

Name: _____ **Date:** _____

Directions: Sort the words in the Word Bank into two categories: *Verbs* and *Nouns*. Write each word in the correct column.

Word Bank				
pursue	noodle	balloon	improve	shampoo
remove	rescue	argue	cartoon	bugle

Verbs	Nouns
○	○
○	○
○	○
○	○
○	○

Directions: Write all 10 words in ABC order.

1. _____   6. _____

2. _____   7. _____

3. _____   8. _____

4. _____   9. _____

5. _____   10. _____

Name: _____ **Date:** _____

Directions: Study how the word changes when you add new endings. Add the same endings to each word to create new words.

1. **approve**   approves   approving   approved

   remove _____   _____   _____

2. **rescue**   rescues   rescuing   rescued

   pursue _____   _____   _____

3. **cruise**   cruises   cruising   cruised

   bruise _____   _____   _____

Directions: Find three words in the Word Bank related to each of the spelling words. Write the words on the correct lines.

Word Bank					
argument	valued	duties	improvement	off-duty	heavy-duty
improving	improved	argued	arguing	valuable	undervalued

4. improve _____   _____   _____

5. argue _____   _____   _____

6. duty _____   _____   _____

7. value _____   _____   _____

Name: _____ **Date:** _____

Directions: Use a word from the Word Bank to complete each analogy.

Word Bank					
argue	balloon	bugle	cartoon	improve	music
nephew	noodles	recruit	remove	rescue	shampoo

Analogies

1. **rolls** is to **ball** as **floats** is to _____

2. **exercise** is to **P.E.** as **sing** is to _____

3. **body** is to **soap** as **hair** is to _____

4. **doctor** is to **heal** as **superhero** is to _____

5. **aunt** is to **uncle** as **niece** is to _____

6. **marinara** is to **sauce** as **spaghetti** is to _____

7. **woodwind** is to **flute** as **brass** is to _____

8. **agree** is to **get along** as **disagree** is to _____

9. **author** is to **book** as **cartoonist** is to _____

10. **buy** is to **advertise** as **join** is to _____

UNIT 21
Schwa Sound

Focus

This week's focus is on the schwa sound in one- and two-syllable words.

Helpful Hint

All the words on this list contain a schwa sound. The schwa sound is pronounced /uh/. In this list, it is represented by *o*, *u*, or *ou*, but can also be represented with *a*, *e*, *i*, or *oo*.

See page 7 for additional spelling activities.

- bulge
- collapse
- collide
- combine
- compete
- complete
- contain
- contrast
- control
- convince
- could've
- insult
- pulse
- result
- should've

Sentence Completions

Name: _____ **Date:**_____

Directions: Use a word from the Word Bank to complete each sentence.

Word Bank					
bulge	collapse	collide	combine	compete	complete
contain	convince	could've	pulse	results	should've

1. Anna can't _____ in the swim meet because she broke her foot.

2. Once I find Ohio and Florida, I will have a _____ set of state quarters.

3. Do these granola bars _____ a lot of sugar?

4. The trains run on separate tracks so they won't _____ .

5. I _____ started studying for my test earlier. Now it's too late.

6. Did Caleb _____ you to let him stay up past his bedtime?

7. You need to _____ the sugar, salt, and flour before you add wet ingredients.

8. I _____ gone shopping with Mom, but I decided to stay home instead.

9. If I build my house of cards too high, it'll definitely _____ .

10. The doctor did some tests on Nana, but we won't get the _____ until tomorrow.

Name: _____ **Date:** _____

Directions: Use a word from the Word Bank to complete each section.

Word Bank					
bulge	collapse	combine	compete	complete	contain
contrast	convince	insult	pulse	result	should've

Write a synonym for each word.

1. heartbeat _____

2. persuade _____

3. mix _____

4. effect _____

Write an antonym for each word.

5. compliment _____

6. not finished _____

7. dent _____

8. compare _____

Write a word that fits each category.

9. crumble, fall apart, cave in, _____

10. could've, would've, you've, _____

11. battle, vie, fight, _____

12. maintain, detain, retain, _____

Prefixes and Suffixes

Name: _____ **Date:** _____

Directions: The prefixes *col–*, *com–*, and *con–* all mean *with* or *together*. Add *col–*, *com–*, or *con–* to each word or root to create a real word.

1. tain _____   6. pete _____

2. lide _____   7. tract _____

3. vince _____   8. pare _____

4. trast _____   9. pose _____

5. bine _____   10. lapse _____

Directions: Choose a word from your answers above to match each description.

11. crash together **with** another moving object _____

12. battle **with** someone in a game or sporting event _____

13. put two things **together** to see how they're the same _____

14. hold things **together** within _____

15. mix things **together** _____

16. a written agreement that people sign **together** _____

Name: _____ **Date:**_____

Directions: Answer each question in a complete sentence. Turn the question around, and use the bold word in your answer.

1. Why do most sandcastles **collapse** at the beach?

   _____

   _____

2. What two flavors would you **combine** to make a new ice cream flavor?

   _____

   _____

3. Why do parents **control** their children's screen time?

   _____

   _____

4. What should you do if you **collide** with another student in line?

   _____

   _____

5. Why is it rude to **insult** your parents' cooking?

   _____

   _____

Turn the Question Around

Analogies

Name: _____   **Date:** _____

Directions: Use a word from the Word Bank to complete each analogy.

Word Bank					
bulge	collapse	collide	combine	compete	complete
contain	contrast	control	insult	pulse	should've

1. **chest** is to **heartbeat** as **wrist** is to _____

2. **could have** is to **could've** as **should have** is to _____

3. **war** is to **fight** as **sporting event** is to _____

4. **push in** is to **dent** as **push out** is to _____

5. **retainer** is to **retain** as **container** is to _____

6. **same** is to **compare** as **different** is to _____

7. **start** is to **begin** as **finish** is to _____

8. **beach umbrella** is to **blow over** as **sandcastle** is to _____

9. **leader** is to **lead** as **controller** is to _____

10. **say nice things** is to **compliment** as **say mean things** is to

_____

UNIT 22

ou/ow Diphthongs

Focus

This week's focus is on *ou* and *ow* diphthongs that appear in two-syllable words and one-syllable words that end with silent *e*.

Helpful Hint

A diphthong, or gliding vowel, starts with one vowel sound and ends with a slightly different vowel sound in the same syllable. *Ou* (*mouth*) and *ow* (*cow*) patterns are two examples. Even though they make the same sound, *ou* only appears in the beginning or middle of a syllable (*bounce*, *hour·ly*). The *ow* pattern can appear at the beginning, middle, or end of a syllable (*chow·der*, *drow·sy*, *al·low*).

See page 7 for additional spelling activities.

- allow
- amount
- blouse
- bounce
- chowder
- devour
- discount
- drowsy
- hourly
- house
- mouse
- pounce
- scrounge
- shower
- spouse

Sentence Completions

Name: _____ Date:_____

Directions: Use a word from the Word Bank to complete each sentence.

Word Bank					
amount	blouse	bounce	chowder	devoured	discount
drowsy	hourly	mouse	scrounged	shower	spouses

1. Mom _____ around the bottom of her purse looking for a pen.

2. When my soccer team came over for dinner, they _____ eight pizzas!

3. Whenever we go to a seafood restaurant, I order a huge bowl of clam

   _____ .

4. If you use this coupon, you'll get a _____ on the price of your haircut.

5. My sister charges _____ for her babysitting services.

6. Save your receipt so I can see the _____ you paid at the grocery store.

7. Are we allowed to bring our _____ to the office party, or is it just for employees?

8. Take a _____ when you're done playing outside, and wash off all that mud.

9. Do I have to wear a dress to the concert, or can I wear nice pants and a

   _____ ?

10. Abby screamed when she saw a _____ nibbling on some cheese in the corner.

Name: _____ **Date:**_____

Directions: Use a word from the Word Bank to complete each section.

Word Bank					
allow	blouse	bounce	chowder	devour	discount
drowsy	hourly	house	pounce	scrounge	spouse

Write a synonym for each word.

1. dribble _____

2. jump toward _____

3. home _____

4. husband or wife _____

Write an antonym for each word.

5. wide awake _____

6. forbid _____

7. nibble at _____

8. price increase _____

Write a word that fits each category.

9. soup, stew, broth, _____

10. daily, monthly, weekly, _____

11. sweater, T-shirt, hoodie, _____

12. dig around, search, look for, _____

Prefixes and Suffixes

Name: _____ **Date:** _____

Directions: The prefix *under–* can mean *not enough* or *below*. Add the prefix *under–* to each word to create a new word.

1. fed _____

2. paid _____

3. cover _____

4. ground _____

5. pass _____

6. water _____

7. wear _____

8. foot _____

9. stand _____

10. go _____

Directions: Choose a word from your answers above to complete each sentence.

11. At last week's lessons, I learned how to swim _____ .

12. We left milk for the stray cat because she looked so _____ .

13. The baby had to _____ surgery for his heart problem.

14. I put away all my clean socks and _____ in the top drawer.

15. You should ask your teacher for help if you don't _____ something.

16. Some animals burrow _____ and stay down there for the winter.

Name: _____ **Date:** _____

Directions: Study how the word changes when you add new endings. Add the same endings to each word to create new words.

1. **pounce**   pounces   pouncing   pounced

   bounce _____ _____ _____

2. **lounge**   lounges   lounging   lounged

   scrounge _____ _____ _____

3. **count**   counts   counting   counted

   discount _____ _____ _____

Directions: Find three words in the Word Bank related to each of the spelling words. Write the words on the correct lines.

Word Bank					
hour	drowsier	allowed	allowance	houses	hours
lighthouse	drowsily	outhouse	drowsiness	hourglass	allowing

4. house   _____ _____ _____

5. allow   _____ _____ _____

6. hourly _____ _____ _____

7. drowsy _____ _____ _____

Name: _____ **Date:** _____

Directions: Use a word from the Word Bank to complete each analogy.

Analogies

Word Bank					
amount	blouse	bounce	chowder	devour	drowsy
hourly	house	mouse	pounce	shower	spouse

1. **zipper** is to **jacket** as **button** is to _____

2. **sit** is to **bath** as **stand** is to _____

3. **brother** is to **sibling** as **husband** is to _____

4. **sip** is to **chug** as **nibble** is to _____

5. **bread crumbs** is to **duck** as **cheese** is to _____

6. **hawk** is to **swoop down** as **cat** is to _____

7. **starving** is to **hungry** as **tired** is to _____

8. **per day** is to **daily** as **per hour** is to _____

9. **rent** is to **apartment** as **own** is to _____

10. **"How big?"** is to **size** as **"How many?"** is to _____

UNIT 23
oi/oy Diphthongs

Focus

This week's focus is on *oi* and *oy* diphthongs that appear in two-syllable words and one-syllable words that end with silent *e*.

Helpful Hint

The diphthongs *oi* (*join*) and *oy* (*toy*) both make the same sound. However, *oi* usually only appears at the beginning or middle of a syllable (*choice*, *oi·ly*). The *oy* pattern only appears at the beginning or end of a syllable (*oy·ster*, *foy·er*, *em·ploy*).

- ➤ **annoy**
- ➤ **appoint**
- ➤ **avoid**
- ➤ **choice**
- ➤ **deploy**
- ➤ **destroy**
- ➤ **employ**
- ➤ **enjoy**
- ➤ **foyer**
- ➤ **joyful**
- ➤ **loiter**
- ➤ **noise**
- ➤ **oily**
- ➤ **rejoice**
- ➤ **voice**

See page 7 for additional spelling activities.

Sentence Completions

Name: _____ Date:_____

Directions: Use a word from the Word Bank to complete each sentence.

Word Bank					
annoy	appoint	avoid	choice	deploy	destroy
employ	foyer	loiter	noise	oily	rejoiced

1. I want a part-time job, but no one will _____ me until I'm 16.

2. Every time I build a tower of blocks, my little brother tries to

   _____ it!

3. When I become president, I will _____ you as my chief of staff.

4. Most stores don't allow anyone to _____ or skateboard on the sidewalk.

5. We had to swerve to _____ the dog that ran out in front of us.

6. Dad told us not to make any _____ because the baby was sleeping.

7. The townspeople _____ when everyone was found alive after the tornado.

8. Nana always keeps a vase of fresh flowers on a table in the

   _____ .

9. Why does my older brother like to _____ me so much?

10. If I don't wash my hair for a couple days, it starts to feel _____ .

Name: _____ **Date:** _____

Directions: Use a word from the Word Bank to complete each section.

Word Bank					
annoy	choice	deploy	destroy	employ	enjoy
foyer	joyful	loiter	noise	oily	rejoice

Write a synonym for each word.

1. hire _____

2. send into battle _____

3. option _____

4. celebrate _____

Write an antonym for each word.

5. silence _____

6. dislike _____

7. build _____

8. sad _____

Write a word that fits each category.

9. bug, bother, pester, _____

10. kitchen, dining room, living room, _____

11. wait around, linger, dawdle, _____

12. greasy, smooth, rough, _____

© Shell Education   28631—180 Days of Spelling and Word Study   145

Inflectional Endings

Name: _____   Date:_____

Directions: Study how the word changes when you add new endings. Add the same endings to each word to create new words.

1. **deploy**   deploys   deploying   deployed

   employ _____   _____   _____

2. **void**   voids   voiding   voided

   avoid _____   _____   _____

3. **point**   points   pointing   pointed

   appoint _____   _____   _____

Directions: Find three words in the Word Bank related to each of the spelling words. Write the words on the correct lines.

Word Bank					
voices	noisy	choose	chosen	voicemail	enjoy
choices	joy	vocal	noises	noisemaker	joyous

4. choice _____   _____   _____

5. voice _____   _____   _____

6. noise _____   _____   _____

7. joyful _____   _____   _____

Name: _____ **Date:** _____

Directions: Answer each question in a complete sentence. Turn the question around, and use the bold word in your answer.

1. What can people do to **avoid** getting sick?

   _____

   _____

2. Why are lunchrooms so **noisy**?

   _____

   _____

3. Why do mosquitoes **annoy** people?

   _____

   _____

4. What are some things you **enjoy** doing at school?

   _____

   _____

5. Why do some stores have "no **loitering**" signs on the sidewalk?

   _____

   _____

Analogies

Name: _____ Date:_____

Directions: Use a word from the Word Bank to complete each analogy.

Word Bank					
annoying	appoint	avoid	choice	deploy	destroy
employ	foyer	loiter	noise	rejoice	voices

1. **band** is to **instruments** as **chorus** is to _____

2. **blindfold** is to **light** as **earplugs** is to _____

3. **president** is to **elect** as **judge** is to _____

4. **building** is to **lobby** as **house** is to _____

5. **waiting room** is to **wait** as **sidewalk** is to _____

6. **police officers** is to **dispatch** as **soldiers** is to _____

7. **decide** is to **decision** as **choose** is to _____

8. **crane** is to **build** as **wrecking ball** is to _____

9. **players** is to **select** as **workers** is to _____

10. **shoulder rub** is to **relaxing** as **shoulder poking** is to _____

UNIT 24

au/aw Digraphs

➤ **autumn**

➤ **caught**

➤ **cause**

➤ **daughter**

➤ **false**

➤ **gauze**

➤ **launch**

➤ **laundry**

➤ **naughty**

➤ **pause**

➤ **sauce**

➤ **swallow**

➤ **taught**

➤ **waffle**

➤ **water**

Focus

This week's focus is on *au* and *aw* digraphs that appear in two-syllable words and one-syllable words that end with silent *e*. A new */aw/* pattern is introduced: *augh*.

Helpful Hint

The digraph *au* (*au·thor*, *au·tumn*) can be found at the beginning or middle of many words but never at the end. Other patterns that make the same sound are *aw*, *augh*, and *al*. The letter *a* can also make the */aw/* sound when it follows *w* (*waf·fle*, *wa·ter*).

See page 7 for additional spelling activities.

Name: _____ **Date:** _____

Directions: Use a word from the Word Bank to complete each sentence.

Word Bank					
autumn	caught	gauze	launch	laundry	naughty
pause	sauce	swallow	taught	waffle	water

1. Can you _____ the movie while I run into the kitchen to get a drink?

2. Do you want another _____ for breakfast?

3. Please put your dirty _____ in the hamper.

4. Chew your meat carefully before you _____ it. I don't want you to choke.

5. When my brother is mean, he gets put on Santa's _____ list.

6. My favorite season is _____ because I like to watch the leaves change color.

7. Do you like to eat your noodles with butter or _____ ?

8. Some people use sprinkler systems to _____ their lawns.

9. I _____ three pop flies during last night's softball game!

10. My dad _____ me how to ride a bike when I was six.

Name: _____ **Date:** _____

Directions: Use a word from the Word Bank to complete each section.

Word Bank					
autumn	cause	daughter	false	gauze	launch
laundry	naughty	pause	sauce	swallow	water

Write a synonym for each word.

1. blast off _____

2. fall _____

3. gulp _____

4. take a break _____

Write an antonym for each word.

5. true _____

6. effect _____

7. son _____

8. well-behaved _____

Write a word that fits each category.

9. gravy, syrup, dressing, _____

10. bandages, medical tape, tweezers, _____

11. juice, milk, coffee, _____

12. cooking, cleaning, yard work, _____

Name: _____ **Date:** _____

Directions: Study how the word changes when you add new endings. Add the same endings to each word to create new words.

1. **pause**   pauses   pausing   paused

   cause   _____   _____   _____

2. **wallow**   wallows   wallowing   wallowed

   swallow _____   _____   _____

3. **taunt**   taunts   taunting   taunted

   haunt   _____   _____   _____

Directions: Find three words in the Word Bank related to each of the spelling words. Write the words on the correct lines.

Word Bank					
teacher	waterfall	saucy	teaches	catcher	watery
teach	catches	catch	saltwater	applesauce	saucepan

4. taught   _____   _____   _____

5. caught   _____   _____   _____

6. sauce   _____   _____   _____

7. water   _____   _____   _____

Name: _____ **Date:**_____

Directions: The prefix *pre–* means *before*. Add the prefix *pre–* to each word or root to create a new word.

1. heat _____
2. school _____
3. pay _____
4. teen _____
5. dict _____

6. fix _____
7. caution _____
8. view _____
9. scribe _____
10. taught _____

Directions: Choose a word from your answers above to complete each sentence.

11. Meteorologists try to _____ the weather, but they're not always accurate.

12. Now that Julianna's a _____ , she wants her own room.

13. Mom's going to _____ the movie to see if it's appropriate for children.

14. Mr. Gardiner put mats under the climbing wall as a _____ .

15. We have to _____ our phone bill, but then we get unlimited data and service.

16. You need to _____ the oven before you bake cookies.

Analogies

Name: _____ **Date:** _____

Directions: Use a word from the Word Bank to complete each analogy.

Word Bank					
autumn	cause	daughter	gauze	launch	laundry
naughty	saucer	swallow	taught	waffles	water

1. **father** is to **mother** as **son** is to _____

2. **catch** is to **caught** as **teach** is to _____

3. **chocolate sauce** is to **sundae** as **syrup** is to _____

4. **dish** is to **placemat** as **teacup** is to _____

5. **volcano** is to **lava** as **fountain** is to _____

6. **tackle box** is to **hooks** as **first aid kit** is to _____

7. **why** is to **because** as **effect** is to _____

8. **air** is to **breathe** as **food** is to _____

9. **plane** is to **take off** as **rocket** is to _____

10. **May** is to **spring** as **September** is to _____

UNIT 25

/aw/ Pattern with ough and oa

Focus

This week's focus is on the /aw/ pattern in one- and two-syllable words. Two new /aw/ patterns are introduced: *ough* and *oa*.

Helpful Hint

The trickiest vowel team in English must be *ou*. It can make a long *o* sound (*dough*), a short *u* sound (*double*), a long *u* sound (*group*), an /ow/ sound (*out*), or an /oo/ sound (*could*). In this week's list, *ou* combines with *gh* to make an /aw/ sound in words such as *bought* and *fought*.

➤ across
➤ bossy
➤ bought
➤ broad
➤ brought
➤ cough
➤ fought
➤ frolic
➤ frosty
➤ lacrosse
➤ offer
➤ often
➤ ought
➤ thought
➤ trough

See page 7 for additional spelling activities.

Name: _____ Date:_____

Directions: Use a word from the Word Bank to complete each sentence.

Word Bank					
across	bought	broad	brought	cough	fought
frolic	lacrosse	offer	often	ought	trough

1. The Northern and Southern states _____ against each other in the Civil War.

2. I _____ my baseball cards in case you want to trade.

3. You don't usually see bats flying around in _____ daylight.

4. My best friend lives _____ the street.

5. We went to the beach and watched children _____ at the water's edge.

6. We don't see my cousins very _____ , only once or twice a year.

7. Next spring, I'd like to play _____ instead of baseball.

8. I just _____ five pairs of socks for you! Where did they all go?

9. You _____ to go outside and play now, before it starts to rain.

10. Thanks for your _____ , but I'm not interested in selling my dolls.

Name: _____ **Date:** _____

Directions: Use a word from the Word Bank to complete each section.

Word Bank					
bossy	bought	broad	cough	frolic	frosty
lacrosse	offer	often	ought	thought	trough

Write a synonym for each word.

1. play _____

2. wondered _____

3. pushy _____

4. purchased _____

Write an antonym for each word.

5. warm _____

6. accept _____

7. shouldn't _____

8. narrow _____

Write a word that fits each category.

9. manger, feed box, food dish, _____

10. sneeze, wheeze, ache, _____

11. tennis, field hockey, golf, _____

12. never, sometimes, rarely, _____

Word Sorts

Name: _____ **Date:**_____

Directions: Sort the words in the Word Bank into two categories: *Past Tense Verbs* and *Present Tense Verbs*. Write each word in the correct column.

Word Bank				
buy	catch	bring	bought	think
brought	fight	fought	thought	caught

Past Tense Verbs	Present Tense Verbs
○	○
○	○
○	○
○	○
○	○

Directions: Write all 10 words in ABC order.

1. _____   6. _____

2. _____   7. _____

3. _____   8. _____

4. _____   9. _____

5. _____   10. _____

Name: _____ **Date:** _____

Directions: Homophones sound the same but have different spellings and meanings. Write the correct homophone on each line.

1. My brother _____ me how to play a new video game.
   (taught/taut)

2. My dad uses his truck to _____ garbage to the dump.
   (hall/haul)

3. I always _____ when I watch that movie because it's so sad.
   (ball/bawl)

4. We trained our puppy to keep her _____ off the furniture.
   (pause/paws)

5. The tailor is going to _____ my pants because they're too long.
   (altar/alter)

6. When you sign a contract, make sure you read each _____ carefully.
   (clause/claws)

7. Eating too much candy can _____ tooth decay and cavities.
   (cause/caws)

8. Koalas use their sharp _____ to climb trees.
   (clause/claws)

9. We had to _____ the movie when someone rang the doorbell.
   (pause/paws)

10. Mom stood in the _____ while she waited for my conference to start.
    (hall/haul)

Analogies

Name: _____ **Date:** _____

Directions: Use a word from the Word Bank to complete each analogy.

Word Bank					
across	bossy	bought	broad	brought	cough
Frosty	lacrosse	often	ought	thought	trough

1. **reindeer** is to **Rudolph** as **snowman** is to _____

2. **head cold** is to **sneeze** as **chest cold** is to _____

3. **dog** is to **dish** as **pig** is to _____

4. **racket** is to **tennis** as **stick** is to _____

5. **thin** is to **narrow** as **wide** is to _____

6. **sing** is to **sang** as **bring** is to _____

7. **drink** is to **drank** as **think** is to _____

8. **"You could…"** is to **helpful** as **"You should…"** is to _____

9. **now** is to **buy** as **yesterday** is to _____

10. **tunnel** is to **through** as **bridge** is to _____

28631—180 Days of Spelling and Word Study   © *Shell Education*

UNIT 26
R-Controlled Vowels with *ar*

Focus

This week's focus is on the /ar/ pattern in one- and two-syllable words.

Helpful Hint

Two rule-breakers on this list are *guard* and *heart*. *Guard* is unusual because it has a silent *u*, which usually only comes before *e* (*guess*), *i* (*guilty*), or *y* (*guy*) to keep the *g* hard. *Heart* is a rule-breaker because it contains *ear*, which never makes an /ar/ sound.

See page 7 for additional spelling activities.

WEEK 26

- army
- artist
- farther
- garlic
- garnish
- guard
- hardly
- heart
- large
- marble
- partner
- party
- remark
- sparkle
- tardy

Sentence Completions

Name: _____ **Date:** _____

Directions: Use a word from the Word Bank to complete each sentence.

Word Bank					
army	garlic	garnish	guard	hardly	hearts
large	marble	party	remark	sparkle	tardy

1. I decorated my parents' Valentine's Day card with lots of bright red

   _____ .

2. Make sure you scrub those dishes until they _____ !

3. I love the taste of _____ , but it gives you bad breath!

4. I got a _____ order of fries and shared them with my friend.

5. Would you like to invite some friends to a _____ for your birthday?

6. We were _____ because the bus broke down on the way to school.

7. I've _____ gotten any sleep this week. My baby brother keeps waking me up!

8. Why did you make that _____ about my funny haircut?

9. Please _____ my dinner while I run upstairs. Make sure the dog doesn't eat it!

10. You can _____ the meal with a sprig of parsley to make it look pretty.

Name: _____ **Date:** _____

Directions: Use a word from the Word Bank to complete each section.

Word Bank					
army	artist	farther	garlic	garnish	guard
hardly	heart	large	remark	sparkle	tardy

Write a synonym for each word.

1. barely _____

2. protect _____

3. decorate a meal _____

4. comment _____

Write an antonym for each word.

5. early _____

6. closer _____

7. look dull _____

8. small _____

Write a word that fits each category.

9. navy, air force, marines, _____

10. brain, lungs, kidneys, _____

11. actor, singer, athlete, _____

12. salt, pepper, chili powder, _____

Name: _____ **Date:** _____

Directions: The suffix *–en* changes an adjective to a verb. Add *–en* to each word to change it from an adjective to a verb. (Remember to drop the silent *e* before you add *–en*.)

1. dark _____
2. sharp _____
3. hard _____
4. soft _____
5. loose _____

6. fresh _____
7. tight _____
8. ripe _____
9. wide _____
10. bright _____

Directions: Choose a word from your answers above to match each description.

11. something you do to a dull knife _____

12. something the sky does when the sun sets _____

13. something the sky does when the sun rises _____

14. something you do to a loose belt _____

15. something hand cream does to your skin _____

16. something that fruit does on a plant or vine _____

Prefixes and Suffixes

Name: _____ **Date:** _____

Directions: Answer each question in a complete sentence. Turn the question around, and use the bold word in your answer.

1. Why are some students **tardy** for school?

   _____

   _____

2. Why do teachers assign students to work with **partners**?

   _____

   _____

3. If you could plan the perfect **party**, what would it be like?

   _____

   _____

4. What are some foods that you love but **hardly** ever eat?

   _____

   _____

5. Why is being a crossing **guard** an important job?

   _____

   _____

Analogies

Name: _____ Date: _____

Directions: Use a word from the Word Bank to complete each analogy.

Word Bank					
army	artist	garlic	garnish	heart	large
marble	partner	party	remark	sparkle	tardy

1. **sailor** is to **navy** as **soldier** is to _____

2. **Thanksgiving** is to **feast** as **birthday** is to _____

3. **gloss** is to **shine** as **glitter** is to _____

4. **smell** is to **nose** as **beat** is to _____

5. **pen** is to **writer** as **paintbrush** is to _____

6. **tiny** is to **small** as **enormous** is to _____

7. **many helpers** is to **group** as **one helper** is to _____

8. **cube** is to **dice** as **sphere** is to _____

9. **chop** is to **onions** as **mince** is to _____

10. **"Where's my hat?"** is to **question** as **"Nice hat!"** is to _____

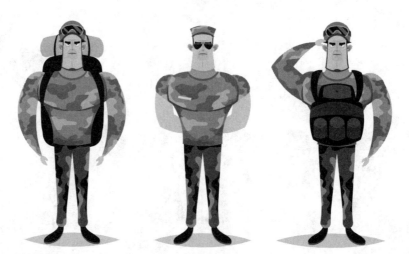

UNIT 27
Long A Patterns with *are*

Focus

This week's focus is on the *are* pattern in one- and two-syllable words.

Helpful Hint

Notice that the silent *e* is dropped when adding a suffix that starts with a vowel (*scary*, *sharing*), but never dropped when adding a suffix that starts with a consonant (*careful*, *barely*).

See page 7 for additional spelling activities.

- aware
- barely
- beware
- careful
- declare
- fare
- glare
- pare
- prepare
- rare
- scary
- share
- spare
- square
- stare

Sentence Completions

Name: _____ **Date:** _____

Directions: Use a word from the Word Bank to complete each sentence.

Word Bank					
aware	barely	beware	careful	declare	fare
pare	prepare	rare	share	spare	squares

1. Let's _____ some of the food now, so we have less to make later.

2. I can _____ see where I'm going. Why is it so dark in here?

3. We should be more _____ of how our actions affect the environment.

4. _____ of my neighbor's dog. He likes to jump on people!

5. Be _____ when you glue the pieces of the vase back together.

6. First, you need to _____ the potatoes. Then, cut them into chunks.

7. How many _____ are on a checkerboard?

8. Do you have a _____ pencil? I can't find any in my desk.

9. Please _____ your markers with Anna so she can finish her project.

10. Do you pay the _____ when you get on the city bus or off it?

Name: _____ **Date:**_____

Directions: Use a word from the Word Bank to complete each section.

Synonyms and Antonyms

Word Bank					
aware	barely	careful	declare	fare	glare
pare	prepare	rare	spare	square	stare

Write a synonym for each word.

1. get ready _____

2. announce_____

3. extra _____

4. hardly _____

Write an antonym for each word.

5. common _____

6. smile _____

7. careless _____

8. oblivious _____

Write a word that fits each category.

9. triangle, circle, rectangle, _____

10. fee, cost, price, _____

11. peel, skin, trim, _____

12. gaze, glimpse, look at, _____

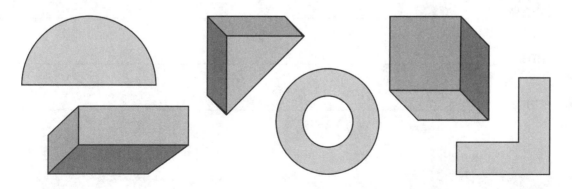

Name: _____ **Date:** _____

Inflectional Endings

Directions: Study how the word changes when you add new endings. Add the same endings to each word to create new words.

1. **care**   cares   caring   cared

   share _____ _____ _____

2. **compare**   compares   comparing   compared

   prepare _____ _____ _____

3. **flare**   flares   flaring   flared

   declare _____ _____ _____

Directions: Find three words in the Word Bank related to each of the spelling words. Write the words on the correct lines.

Word Bank					
airfare	scare	care	bare	bus fare	scared
barefoot	farewell	careless	threadbare	caretaker	scarecrow

4. careful _____ _____ _____

5. barely _____ _____ _____

6. fare _____ _____ _____

7. scary _____ _____ _____

Name: _____ **Date:** _____

Directions: Sort the words in the Word Bank into two categories: *Verbs* and *Adjectives*. Write each word in the correct column.

Word Bank				
glare	rare	square	prepare	scary
stare	declare	careful	share	aware

Verbs	Adjectives
○	○
○	○
○	○
○	○
○	○

Directions: Write all 10 words in ABC order.

1. _____   6. _____

2. _____   7. _____

3. _____   8. _____

4. _____   9. _____

5. _____   10. _____

Analogies

Name: _____ Date:_____

Directions: Use a word from the Word Bank to complete each analogy.

Word Bank					
barely	beware	declare	fare	glare	prepare
rare	scary	share	spare	square	stare

1. **happy** is to **smile** as **angry** is to _____

2. **comedy** is to **funny** as **horror film** is to _____

3. **too much** is to **plenty** as **just enough** is to _____

4. **hear** is to **listen** as **see** is to _____

5. **three sides** is to **triangle** as **four sides** is to _____

6. **stone** is to **common** as **diamond** is to _____

7. **table** is to **set** as **dinner** is to _____

8. **plan** is to **back-up** as **tire** is to _____

9. **mail** is to **postage** as **people** is to _____

10. **friendly dogs** is to **approach** as **mean dogs** is to _____

28631—180 Days of Spelling and Word Study   © *Shell Education*

UNIT 28

Long A Patterns with *air* and *ear*

Focus

This week's focus is on the *air* and *ear* patterns in one- and two-syllable words.

Helpful Hint

Some words on this list are homophones, which means they sound the same but have different spellings and meanings (*bear/bare*, *fairy/ferry*, *pear/pair*, *wear/where*). The word *tear* is a *heterophone* because it represents two words that have the same spelling but different meanings and pronunciations (*tēr/tār*).

- airplane
- bear
- dairy
- despair
- fairground
- fairy
- impair
- pear
- prairie
- repair
- staircase
- swear
- tear
- wear
- wheelchair

See page 7 for additional spelling activities.

Name: _____ Date:_____

Sentence Completions

Directions: Use a word from the Word Bank to complete each sentence.

Word Bank					
airplane	dairy	despair	fairground	fairy	impair
pears	prairie	repair	swear	tear	wheelchair

1. Do you _____ that you didn't touch my Halloween candy?

2. My uncle owns a _____ farm in Vermont. Sometimes, he lets me milk the cows.

3. Don't _____ . We'll figure out a way to get home!

4. Mom's hand lotion smells like fresh _____ .

5. Some medicines can _____ your ability to drive a car safely.

6. I've never flown on an _____ before. Have you?

7. Many settlers moved to the _____ because of its rich soil.

8. Can you _____ the washing machine, or do we need to buy a new one?

9. Do you think the tooth _____ will come tonight?

10. Just _____ out these three pages, and then you'll have a brand new notebook!

28631—*180 Days of Spelling and Word Study*

Name: _____ **Date:** _____

Directions: Use a word from the Word Bank to complete each section.

Word Bank					
bear	dairy	despair	fairy	impair	pear
prairie	repair	swear	tear	wear	wheelchair

Write a synonym for each word.

1. grassland _____

2. pixie   _____

3. take an oath _____

4. dress in   _____

Write an antonym for each word.

5. break   _____

6. tape together _____

7. keep hoping _____

8. strengthen _____

Write a word that fits each category.

9. apple, peach, plum, _____

10. deer, wolf, raccoon, _____

11. protein, grains, vegetables, _____

12. crutches, cane, scooter, _____

Inflectional Endings

Name: _____ **Date:** _____

Directions: Study how the word changes when you add new endings. Add the same endings to each word to create new words.

1. **tear**   tears   tearing   tore

   swear   _____   _____   _____

   wear   _____   _____   _____

2. **despair**   despairs   despairing   despaired

   impair   _____   _____

   repair   _____   _____

Directions: Find three words in the Word Bank related to each of the spelling words. Write the words on the correct lines.

Word Bank					
air	repairable	stair	airline	chairlift	chair
stairwell	repairman	disrepair	chairman	airbag	downstairs

3. wheelchair _____   _____   _____

4. repair   _____   _____   _____

5. staircase _____   _____   _____

6. airplane _____   _____   _____

Name: _____ **Date:** _____

Directions: Homophones sound the same but have different spellings and meanings. Write the correct homophone on each line.

1. We saw a brown _____ when we went camping in the woods.
   (bare/bear)

2. Is $2.00 enough to pay for my bus _____ ?
   (fair/fare)

3. I always _____ my lucky socks when I have a math test.
   (wear/where)

4. Don't walk near the broken glass if your feet are _____ .
   (bare/bear)

5. Have you read the story about the tortoise and the _____ ?
   (hair/hare)

6. When a famous person walks into the restaurant, everyone stops and

   _____ .
   (stairs/stares)

7. Judges are not allowed to choose sides. They must always be

   _____ .
   (fair/fare)

8. Bring an extra _____ of socks in case these get wet.
   (pair/pare/pear)

9. Would you like an apple or a _____ in your lunchbox?
   (pair/pare/pear)

10. Mom said I have to cut my _____ because it's hanging
    in my eyes.
    (hair/hare)

© Shell Education

Name: _____ **Date:** _____

Directions: Use a word from the Word Bank to complete each analogy.

Word Bank					
airplane	bear	dairy	despair	fairground	fairy
impair	pears	prairie	repair	wear	wheelchair

1. **bread** is to **grain** as **milk** is to _____

2. **Captain Hook** is to **pirate** as **Tinker Bell** is to _____

3. **umbrella** is to **carry** as **raincoat** is to _____

4. **vine** is to **grapes** as **tree** is to _____

5. **staircase** is to **feet** as **ramp** is to _____

6. **captain** is to **ship** as **pilot** is to _____

7. **bird** is to **owl** as **mammal** is to _____

8. **baseball game** is to **stadium** as **fair** is to _____

9. **installer** is to **install** as **repairman** is to _____

10. **dry** is to **desert** as **grassy** is to _____

UNIT 29

R-Controlled Vowels with *or*

Focus

This week's focus is on the *or* pattern in two-syllable words.

Helpful Hint

All the words on this list contain *r*-controlled syllables. *R*-controlled syllables have a vowel followed by the letter *r*. When dividing these words into syllables, split them after the prefix (*re·port*, *per·form*) or after the *r*-controlled chunk (*stor·my*, *bor·der*).

➤ acorn
➤ border
➤ forty
➤ import
➤ morning
➤ northern
➤ order
➤ perform
➤ popcorn
➤ record
➤ reform
➤ report
➤ stormy
➤ story
➤ transport

See page 7 for additional spelling activities.

Name: _____   **Date:** _____

Directions: Use a word from the Word Bank to complete each sentence.

Sentence Completions

Word Bank					
acorns	border	import	morning	order	perform
record	reform	report	stormy	story	transport

1. Did you see that beautiful sunrise this _____ ?

2. The huge oak tree dropped _____ all over our front lawn.

3. Please _____ your message at the beep.

4. Truck drivers _____ goods to warehouses and stores across the country.

5. We need to _____ our laws to make people safer.

6. Let's head home from the beach. The sky looks _____ .

7. I need to finish my _____ on polar bears by Friday.

8. Would you like to _____ some Girl Scout cookies?

9. Watch me _____ this magic trick!

10. What other countries _____ France besides Spain?

Name: _____ **Date:** _____

Directions: Use a word from the Word Bank to complete each section.

Word Bank					
acorns	border	forty	import	morning	northern
popcorn	record	reform	stormy	story	transport

Write a synonym for each word.

1. carry _____

2. tale _____

3. edge _____

4. improve _____

Write an antonym for each word.

5. southern _____

6. export _____

7. evening _____

8. erase _____

Write a word that fits each category.

9. rainy, windy, sunny, _____

10. pine cones, maple seeds, coconuts, _____

11. pretzels, chips, crackers, _____

12. twenty, ninety, eighty, _____

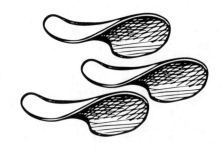

Name: _____   Date:_____

Prefixes and Suffixes

Directions: The prefix *re–* means *again*. Add the prefix *re–* to each word or root to create a new word.

1. form   _____

2. port   _____

3. cord   _____

4. tell   _____

5. build   _____

6. fill   _____

7. finish   _____

8. act   _____

9. send   _____

10. enter   _____

Directions: Choose a word from your answers above to complete each sentence.

11. Families had to _____ their homes after the hurricane struck.

12. Dad went to the pharmacy to _____ my prescription.

13. My first email didn't go through, so I had to _____ it.

14. Can you _____ this show so I can watch it later?

15. We have to _____ the story and then draw a picture to go with it.

16. Find out what happened, and then _____ back to us.

Name: _____ **Date:** _____

Directions: Answer each question in a complete sentence. Turn the question around, and use the bold word in your answer.

1. What do you like to do on Saturday **mornings**?

   _____

   _____

2. What kinds of things can people **order** online?

   _____

   _____

3. How does your family **transport** food from the grocery store?

   _____

   _____

4. What will you have when you're **forty**?

   _____

   _____

5. What do you like to put on your **popcorn**?

   _____

   _____

Analogies

Name: _____ **Date:** _____

Directions: Use a word from the Word Bank to complete each analogy.

Word Bank					
acorns	borders	forty	import	morning	northern
perform	popcorn	record	stormy	story	transport

1. **6:00 p.m.** is to **evening** as **6:00 a.m.** is to _____

2. **puffy clouds** is to **sunny** as **dark clouds** is to _____

3. **penguins** is to **southern** as **polar bears** is to _____

4. **palm tree** is to **coconuts** as **oak tree** is to _____

5. **paper** is to **edges** as **country** is to _____

6. **scene** is to **photograph** as **voice** is to _____

7. **sing** is to **lullaby** as **read** is to _____

8. **soccer** is to **play** as **gymnastics** is to _____

9. **bulldozer** is to **dig** as **dump truck** is to _____

10. **three tens** is to **thirty** as **four tens** is to _____

UNIT 30

R-Controlled Vowels with *oar*, *oor*, *our*, and *ore*

Focus

This week's focus is on the *oar*, *oor*, *our*, and *ore* patterns in one- and two-syllable words.

Helpful Hint

Many of the words on this list are homophones (*board/bored*, *course/coarse*, *horse/hoarse*, *soar/sore*). Only one form of each word is included on this list. Take some time to learn its spelling and meaning thoroughly in context before memorizing the second spelling and meaning.

➤ board
➤ course
➤ court
➤ divorce
➤ door
➤ enforce
➤ explore
➤ floor
➤ force
➤ horse
➤ ignore
➤ poor
➤ roar
➤ soar
➤ source

See page 7 for additional spelling activities.

Name: _____ **Date:** _____

Directions: Use a word from the Word Bank to complete each sentence.

Word Bank					
board	course	court	divorce	door	enforce
floor	horse	ignore	poor	soar	source

Sentence Completions

1. You need to take a driving _____ before you can get your license.

2. I just _____ my brother when he starts acting goofy.

3. I found the _____ of that horrible smell. There's rotten meat in the trash!

4. I dropped a jar of jam on the _____ and it smashed.

5. We keep our _____ at a neighbor's farm and ride him whenever we can.

6. Remember to copy your homework off the _____ as soon as you come into class.

7. My dad went to _____ to fight a speeding ticket.

8. We sent books and shoes to _____ children in need.

9. I wish I could _____ like a bird high up in the sky.

10. Please close the _____ so cold air doesn't get in.

Name: _____ **Date:** _____

Directions: Use a word from the Word Bank to complete each section.

Synonyms and Antonyms

Word Bank					
board	court	divorce	door	explore	floor
force	horse	ignore	poor	roar	soar

Write a synonym for each word.

1. fly high _____

2. search _____

3. require _____

4. bellow _____

Write an antonym for each word.

5. rich _____

6. pay attention _____

7. ceiling _____

8. marry _____

Write a word that fits each category.

9. cow, pig, donkey, _____

10. window, staircase, chimney, _____

11. two-by-four, plank, beam, _____

12. field, course, rink, _____

Inflectional Endings

Name: _____ **Date:** _____

Directions: Study how the word changes when you add new endings. Add the same endings to each word to create new words.

1. **adore**   adores   adoring   adored

   explore _____   _____   _____

   ignore _____   _____   _____

2. **force**   forces   forcing   forced

   enforce _____   _____   _____

   divorce _____   _____   _____

Directions: Find three words in the Word Bank related to each of the spelling words. Write the words on the correct lines.

Word Bank					
doorknob	horseshoe	seahorse	cardboard	doorbell	courthouse
courtroom	chalkboard	doorway	racehorse	courts	whiteboard

3. board   _____   _____   _____

4. court   _____   _____   _____

5. door   _____   _____   _____

6. horse   _____   _____   _____

Name: _____ **Date:**_____

Directions: Homophones sound the same but have different spellings and meanings. Write the correct homophone on each line.

1. My muscles were _____ after I helped Dad shovel the driveway. **(soar/sore)**

2. Can you please _____ me a glass of milk? **(poor/pour)**

3. I wish I could _____ through the air like a bird! **(soar/sore)**

4. When I was younger, my parents were too _____ to buy a car. **(poor/pour)**

5. Have you ever ridden on a _____ before? **(hoarse/horse)**

6. My hair is thin and fine, but my sister's is thick and _____ . **(coarse/course)**

7. I screamed so much at the football game that my voice grew

   _____ . **(hoarse/horse)**

8. Please copy your homework neatly from the _____ . **(board/bored)**

9. I have _____ sisters and one brother. **(four/for)**

10. I baked these cookies especially _____ you! **(four/for)**

Analogies

Name: _____ **Date:** _____

Directions: Use a word from the Word Bank to complete each analogy.

Word Bank					
course	court	divorce	door	explore	floor
horse	ignore	poor	roar	soar	source

1. **wallpaper** is to **wall** as **rug** is to _____

2. **wolf** is to **howl** as **lion** is to _____

3. **baseball** is to **field** as **basketball** is to _____

4. **grass** is to **cow** as **oats** is to _____

5. **look out** is to **window** as **walk out** is to _____

6. **date** is to **break up** as **marry** is to _____

7. **mansion** is to **rich** as **shack** is to _____

8. **voyager** is to **voyage** as **explorer** is to _____

9. **downhill** is to **coast** as **through the air** is to _____

10. **hockey** is to **rink** as **golf** is to _____

UNIT 31
R-Controlled Vowels with *quar*, *war*, and *wor*

Focus

This week's focus is on *quar*, *war*, and *wor* patterns in one- and two-syllable words.

Helpful Hint

Notice that *ar* takes on a new sound when it follows *qu* or *w*. It sounds like /or/ in words such as *war* and *quarter*. Meanwhile, *or* changes to an /er/ sound when it follows *w* in words such as *work* and *worth*.

> See page 7 for additional spelling activities.

- quart
- quarter
- war
- ward
- warm
- warn
- wart
- work
- world
- worm
- worry
- worse
- worst
- worth
- worthless

Name: _____ **Date:** _____

Directions: Use a word from the Word Bank to complete each sentence.

Word Bank					
quart	quarter	ward	warm	warn	wart
world	worry	worse	worst	worth	worthless

1. It's getting very _____ in here. Can you open the window?

2. How much is this old car _____ ?

3. When I grow up, I'm going to travel all over the _____ .

4. Don't _____ about the mess. I'll clean it up later.

5. We visited my aunt and her new baby in the maternity _____ of the hospital.

6. The coach gave his team a quick pep talk after the first _____ .

7. I had the _____ night's sleep. I just kept tossing and turning!

8. Mom told me to throw away this _____ piece of junk.

9. Dad asked us to pick up a _____ of coffee creamer at the supermarket.

10. If your cough gets _____ , we should bring you to the doctor.

Name: _____   Date:_____

Directions: Use a word from the Word Bank to complete each section.

Word Bank					
quarter	war	ward	warm	warn	wart
work	world	worm	worse	worst	worth

Write a synonym for each word.

1. Earth   _____

2. value   _____

3. notify   _____

4. most awful _____

Write an antonym for each word.

5. peace   _____

6. play   _____

7. chilly   _____

8. better   _____

Write a word that fits each category.

9. penny, dime, nickel, _____

10. pimple, mole, birthmark, _____

11. department, unit, section, _____

12. caterpillar, centipede, snake, _____

Name: _____ **Date:** _____

Directions: The prefix *inter–* means *between* or *among*. Add the prefix *inter–* to each word or root to create a real word.

1. com _____

2. rupt _____

3. state _____

4. view _____

5. cept _____

6. mission _____

7. fere _____

8. national _____

9. section _____

10. pret _____

Directions: Choose a word from your answers above to match each description.

11. a short break **between** parts of a play _____

12. travel **between** two or more countries _____

13. a highway that goes **between** two or more states _____

14. a device that is used to communicate **between** classrooms or offices

_____

15. a place where two roads cross, allowing you to travel **between** them

_____

Name: _____ **Date:**_____

Directions: Answer each question in a complete sentence. Turn the question around, and use the bold word in your answer.

1. Why do children **worry** about moving to new schools?

   _____

   _____

2. What's the **worst** food you've ever tasted?

   _____

   _____

3. Why do parents **warn** their children to look both ways before they cross the street?

   _____

   _____

4. Why do bug bites get **worse** when you scratch them?

   _____

   _____

5. Why should students **work** hard at school?

   _____

   _____

Turn the Question Around

Analogies

Name: _____ **Date:** _____

Directions: Use a word from the Word Bank to complete each analogy.

Word Bank					
quart	quarter	war	wards	warm	warts
work	world	worm	worry	worst	worthless

1. **slither** is to **snake** as **wriggle** is to _____

2. **ambulance** is to **emergency** as **tank** is to _____

3. **iced tea** is to **cold** as **cocoa** is to _____

4. **"I hope…"** is to **wish** as **"What if…"** is to _____

5. **weekend** is to **relax** as **weekday** is to _____

6. **better** is to **best** as **worse** is to _____

7. **milk** is to **gallon** as **heavy cream** is to _____

8. **national** is to **country** as **global** is to _____

9. **school** is to **wings** as **hospital** is to _____

10. **sun's rays** is to **sunburn** as **virus** is to _____

UNIT 32

R-Controlled Vowels with *er*

Focus

This week's focus is on *er* patterns in one- and two-syllable words.

Helpful Hint

Silent *e* appears at the end of many words on this list, but it doesn't serve the usual purpose of making vowels long. Instead, it softens the *g* (*merge*), keeps *v* company at the end of a word (*serve*, *nerve*), and helps *s* maintain its own sound, since *s* usually sounds like *z* after an *r*-controlled vowel (*verse*, *reverse*).

- alert
- danger
- desert
- every
- germs
- merge
- nerve
- never
- pattern
- prefer
- reverse
- serve
- stranger
- swerve
- verse

See page 7 for additional spelling activities.

Name: _____ **Date:** _____

Directions: Use a word from the Word Bank to complete each sentence.

Word Bank					
alert	danger	desert	germs	merge	nerve
pattern	prefer	reverse	serve	swerve	verse

1. Do you like the striped _____ on this dress?

2. I would love to go to the _____ to see cactuses, owls, and lizards.

3. My mom gets an _____ on her phone every time there's a tornado warning.

4. Remember to use your blinker every time you _____ into traffic.

5. We had to _____ to avoid the squirrel when it ran onto the road.

6. I can only sing the first _____ of *America the Beautiful*.

7. When animals sense _____ in the forest, they run away.

8. I _____ chocolate ice cream, but vanilla is tasty too.

9. Put the car in _____ , and then back out of the driveway.

10. Do they _____ pizza by the slice here, or do you have to buy a whole pie?

Name: _____ Date:_____

Directions: Use a word from the Word Bank to complete each section.

Word Bank					
alert	danger	desert	every	merge	nerves
never	pattern	prefer	reverse	stranger	verse

Synonyms and Antonyms

Write a synonym for each word.

1. warn _____

2. come together _____

3. design _____

4. like better _____

Write an antonym for each word.

5. go forward _____

6. safety _____

7. none _____

8. always _____

Write a word that fits each category.

9. prairie, jungle, forest, _____

10. brain, spinal cord, neurons, _____

11. stanza, paragraph, chapter, _____

12. outsider, foreigner, unknown person, _____

Name: _____ **Date:** _____

Directions: The prefix *over–* means *above* or *too much*. Add the prefix *over–* to each word to create a new word.

1. do   _____   6. dose   _____

2. due   _____   7. sleep   _____

3. head   _____   8. cooked _____

4. reacts   _____   9. weight _____

5. time   _____   10. charged _____

Directions: Choose a word from your answers above to complete each sentence.

11. If I don't set my alarm, I will probably _____ tomorrow.

12. Dad had to work _____ because he had so many jobs to finish.

13. Check the receipt. I think the store _____ us.

14. I forgot to take the cake out of the oven. Now it's _____ .

15. Mom used a ladder to change the _____ lights.

16. Let's stop by the library to return our _____ books.

Name: _____ **Date:** _____

Directions: Study how the word changes when you add new endings. Add the same endings to each word to create new words.

1. **refer**   refers   referring   referred

   prefer _____ _____ _____

2. **swerve**   swerves   swerving   swerved

   serve   _____ _____ _____

3. **desert**   deserts   deserting   deserted

   alert   _____ _____ _____

Directions: Find three words in the Word Bank related to each of the spelling words. Write the words on the correct lines.

Word Bank					
reversal	merging	strange	reversed	merged	dangerous
strangely	dangers	merges	reversing	strangest	endanger

4. danger _____ _____ _____

5. reverse _____ _____ _____

6. stranger _____ _____ _____

7. merge _____ _____ _____

Analogies

Name: _____   Date:_____

Directions: Use a word from the Word Bank to complete each analogy.

Word Bank					
alert	desert	every	germs	merge	nerves
pattern	reverse	serve	stranger	swerve	verse

1. **pine tree** is to **forest** as **cactus** is to _____

2. **poem** is to **stanza** as **song** is to _____

3. **fuzzy** is to **texture** as **polka dotted** is to _____

4. **baseball** is to **pitch** as **tennis ball** is to _____

5. **go forward** is to **drive** as **go backward** is to _____

6. **heart** is to **blood vessels** as **brain** is to _____

7. **familiar** is to **friend** as **unfamiliar** is to _____

8. **alarm clock** is to **awaken** as **smoke alarm** is to _____

9. **healthy** is to **vitamins** as **sick** is to _____

10. **none** is to **not any** as **all** is to _____

UNIT 33
R-Controlled Vowels with *ur*

Focus

This week's focus is on *ur* patterns in one- and two-syllable words.

Helpful Hint

Silent *e* appears again at the end of many of these words. It softens the *g* (*urge*), keeps *v* company at the end of a word (*curve*), and helps *s* maintain its own sound, since *s* usually sounds like *z* after an *r*-controlled vowel (*furs*, *nurse*, *purse*).

- blurry
- cure
- curse
- curve
- disturb
- during
- hurry
- nurse
- pure
- purple
- purse
- sturdy
- surprise
- turtle
- urge

🔍 See page 7 for additional spelling activities.

Name: _____ **Date:** _____

Directions: Use a word from the Word Bank to complete each sentence.

Word Bank					
cures	curse	curve	disturb	during	hurry
nurse	pure	purple	purse	sturdy	surprise

Sentence Completions

1. Was your aunt's baby shower a _____ , or did she know about it?

2. The school _____ can give you an ice pack for your bruised knee.

3. No talking is allowed _____ the test.

4. Please _____ so you don't miss the bus.

5. Would you like green or _____ bands for your braces?

6. After the blizzard, everything was covered with _____ white snow.

7. Try not to _____ your sister. She's studying for a big test.

8. The witch put a _____ on the man, and it changed him into a turtle.

9. When I grow up, I want to develop _____ for diseases.

10. Do you carry a _____ to school, or do you throw everything in your backpack?

Name: _____ **Date:** _____

Directions: Use a word from the Word Bank to complete each section.

Synonyms and Antonyms

Word Bank					
blurry	cure	curse	disturb	during	hurry
pure	purple	purse	sturdy	turtle	urge

Write a synonym for each word.

1. rush _____

2. heal _____

3. bother _____

4. persuade _____

Write an antonym for each word.

5. flimsy _____

6. blessing _____

7. clear _____

8. polluted _____

Write a word that fits each category.

9. handbag, backpack, duffel bag, _____

10. orange, green, yellow, _____

11. before, after, a while ago, _____

12. lizard, snake, alligator, _____

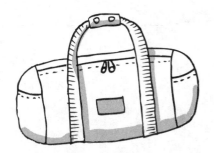

Word Sorts

Name: _____ **Date:**_____

Directions: Sort the words in the Word Bank into two categories: *Adjectives* and *Verbs*. Write each word in the correct column.

Word Bank				
sturdy	urge	cure	blurry	purple
surprise	pure	curvy	curse	disturb

Adjectives	Verbs
○	○
○	○
○	○
○	○
○	○

Directions: Write all 10 words in ABC order.

1. _____   6. _____

2. _____   7. _____

3. _____   8. _____

4. _____   9. _____

5. _____   10. _____

Name: _____ **Date:**_____

Directions: Answer each question in a complete sentence. Turn the question around, and use the bold word in your answer.

1. Why should a tree house be built on **sturdy** branches?

   _____

   _____

2. How does a **turtle** protect itself?

   _____

   _____

3. What should students do **during** a fire drill?

   _____

   _____

4. Why is it rude to **disturb** people who are taking a test?

   _____

   _____

5. What's the best way to **cure** a case of hiccups?

   _____

   _____

Name: _____ **Date:**_____

Directions: Use a word from the Word Bank to complete each analogy.

Analogies

Word Bank					
cure	curves	disturb	hurry	nurse	pure
purple	purse	sturdy	surprised	turtle	urge

1. **dollar bills** is to **wallet** as **coins** is to _____

2. **safety** is to **officer** as **health** is to _____

3. **apple** is to **red** as **grape** is to _____

4. **quills** is to **porcupine** as **shell** is to _____

5. **X** is to **straight lines** as **S** is to _____

6. **plastic fork** is to **flimsy** as **metal fork** is to _____

7. **tiptoe in** is to **not interrupt** as **barge in** is to _____

8. **lips quiver** is to **scared** as **jaw drops** is to _____

9. **injury** is to **heal** as **disease** is to _____

10. **brown snow** is to **dirty** as **white snow** is to _____

UNIT 34

R-Controlled Vowels with *ear* and *ir*

- birthday
- circle
- dirty
- early
- earn
- earth
- firmly
- heard
- learn
- pearl
- rehearse
- search
- thirsty
- thirty
- yearn

Focus

This week's focus is on *ear* and *ir* patterns in one- and two-syllable words.

Helpful Hint

There are many ways to spell the /er/ sound in English: *er, ir, or, ur, ear*, and others. Make a mental picture of each word as you study it, so you know which spelling just "looks right." It's also helpful to learn words in batches so you know which words share the same pattern.

See page 7 for additional spelling activities.

Name: _____ Date:_____

Directions: Use a word from the Word Bank to complete each sentence.

Word Bank					
circle	dirty	earn	Earth	firmly	heard
learn	pearl	rehearse	search	thirsty	yearn

1. Can you help me _____ for my car keys?

2. Your hands are so _____ ! Wash them before you sit down to eat.

3. My grandmother left me a beautiful _____ necklace when she died.

4. I _____ about the fire at the old factory yesterday.

5. We need to _____ for a couple weeks, and then we'll be ready to perform.

6. As satellites orbit _____ , they send signals from one antenna to another.

7. I'm so _____ , I could drink a whole gallon of water right now!

8. When my house gets noisy, I _____ for peace and quiet.

9. The teacher told us to sit in a _____ so we could pass around the photos.

10. This summer, I'm going to _____ how to sail at summer camp!

Name: _____ **Date:** _____

Directions: Use a word from the Word Bank to complete each section.

Word Bank					
circle	dirty	early	earn	Earth	firmly
learn	pearl	rehearse	search	thirty	yearn

Write a synonym for each word.

1. seek _____

2. get paid _____

3. crave _____

4. practice _____

Write an antonym for each word.

5. late _____

6. loosely _____

7. clean _____

8. teach _____

Write a word that fits each category.

9. diamond, emerald, ruby, _____

10. square, trapezoid, hexagon, _____

11. Jupiter, Venus, Mars, _____

12. twenty, fifty, eighty, _____

Name: _____ Date:_____

Directions: Study how the word changes when you add new endings. Add the same endings to each word to create new words.

1. **yearn**   yearns   yearning   yearned

    learn   _____   _____   _____

    earn   _____   _____   _____

2. **whir**   whirs   whirring   whirred

    stir   _____   _____   _____

Directions: Find three words in the Word Bank related to each of the spelling words. Write the words on the correct lines.

Word Bank					
earliest	rehearsal	earthworm	thirst	rehearsing	earlier
thirstier	earthquake	thirstiest	rehearsed	early bird	earthly

3. earth   _____   _____   _____

4. thirsty   _____   _____   _____

5. early   _____   _____   _____

6. rehearse   _____   _____   _____

Inflectional Endings

Name: _____   **Date:** _____

Directions: Homophones sound the same but have different spellings and meanings. Write the correct homophone on each line.

1. Have you _____ of a woman named Nellie Bly?
    (heard/herd)

2. We have a lot of _____ trees growing in our backyard.
    (fir/fur)

3. My cousin has been blind since _____ .
    (berth/birth)

4. I had to pay a fee at the library since my books were _____ .
    (overdo/overdue)

5. Remember you just got off crutches. Don't _____ it in gym class today.
    (overdo/overdue)

6. I like to fall asleep listening to the _____ of the ceiling fan in my bedroom.
    (were/whir)

7. I love to pet my kitten's _____ .
    (fir/fur)

8. My grandparents _____ late because they stopped to pick up treats for us.
    (were/whir)

9. The Apache tribe followed a _____ of buffalo across the plains.
    (heard/herd)

10. My mom _____ five other employees at her new job.
    (oversees/overseas)

Analogies

Name: _____ **Date:** _____

Directions: Use a word from the Word Bank to complete each analogy.

Word Bank					
birthday	circle	dirty	early	earn	Earth
heard	learn	pearl	rehearse	thirsty	thirty

1. **eyes** is to **saw** as **ears** is to _____

2. **11:00 p.m.** is to **late** as **5:00 a.m.** is to _____

3. **nap** is to **tired** as **bath** is to _____

4. **gift** is to **receive** as **paycheck** is to _____

5. **candy** is to **Halloween** as **present** is to _____

6. **rectangular** is to **rectangle** as **round** is to _____

7. **ring** is to **diamond** as **necklace** is to _____

8. **eight tens** is to **eighty** as **three tens** is to _____

9. **hospital** is to **heal** as **school** is to _____

10. **snack** is to **hungry** as **cold drink** is to _____

UNIT 35
–tion Ending

Focus

This week's focus is on the *–tion* ending in two-syllable words.

Helpful Hint

All words that end with *–tion* are nouns. Some *–tion* endings can be used as verbs as well. For example, use caution (noun) when you look both ways before crossing the street. You can also caution (verb) someone when you tell them to look both ways. *Auction*, *mention*, *question*, and *section* can also be used as nouns and verbs.

- ➤ **action**
- ➤ **auction**
- ➤ **caption**
- ➤ **caution**
- ➤ **fiction**
- ➤ **fraction**
- ➤ **lotion**
- ➤ **mention**
- ➤ **motion**
- ➤ **nation**
- ➤ **option**
- ➤ **potion**
- ➤ **question**
- ➤ **section**
- ➤ **station**

See page 7 for additional spelling activities.

Sentence Completions

Name: _____ Date: _____

Directions: Use a word from the Word Bank to complete each sentence.

Word Bank					
auction	caption	caution	fiction	fraction	lotion
mention	nation	option	potion	section	station

1. Do you have any _____ left? My hands are very dry.

2. I prefer to read _____ , but my brother loves books about real things.

3. My parents brought me to an _____ and let me bid on pieces of art.

4. You don't need a passport to visit any states in the _____ .

5. Can you hand me the sports _____ so I can read about last night's game?

6. If I eat $\frac{1}{4}$ of the pie and Andrew eats $\frac{1}{4}$ of the pie, what _____ is left?

7. I forgot to _____ that tomorrow is an early dismissal day.

8. I don't want to show up late for the party, but I don't have any other

   _____ .

9. Dad had to go to the police _____ to get fingerprinted for his new job.

10. If you read the _____ , it'll tell you what kind of lizard is in the photograph.

28631—180 Days of Spelling and Word Study

Name: _____ **Date:** _____

Directions: Use a word from the Word Bank to complete each section.

Word Bank					
caption	caution	fiction	lotion	mention	motion
nation	option	potion	question	section	station

Write a synonym for each word.

1. choice _____

2. talk about _____

3. movement _____

4. country _____

Write an antonym for each word.

5. nonfiction _____

6. answer _____

7. whole _____

8. recklessness _____

Write a word that fits each category.

9. heading, glossary, photograph, _____

10. cream, gel, moisturizer, _____

11. mixture, brew, concoction, _____

12. headquarters, office, base, _____

Name: _____ **Date:** _____

Directions: The prefix *trans–* means *across* or *through*. Add the prefix *trans–* to each word or root to create a new word.

1. port _____

2. action _____

3. atlantic _____

4. continental _____

5. form _____

6. plant _____

7. form _____

8. late _____

9. parent _____

10. mits _____

Directions: Choose a word from your answers above to complete each sentence.

11. Matt started his _____ journey in New York and finished in California.

12. We rented a moving van to _____ all our furniture to the new house.

13. My uncle needs a kidney _____ . I hope they find a donor soon.

14. They won't let you complete a _____ at the bank unless you show ID.

15. I love to watch caterpillars _____ into butterflies!

16. Windows are made of a _____ material so you can see through them.

Name: _____ **Date:** _____

Directions: Answer each question in a complete sentence. Turn the question around, and use the bold word in your answer.

1. Why is it important to read **captions**?

   _____

   _____

2. Why is **fiction** so much fun to read?

   _____

   _____

3. Why do people put **lotion** on their hands?

   _____

   _____

4. Why is it important to use **caution** when you're cooking?

   _____

   _____

5. Why is it important to ask your teacher **questions**?

   _____

   _____

Name: _____ **Date:** _____

Directions: Use a word from the Word Bank to complete each analogy.

Word Bank					
action	auction	caption	fiction	fraction	lotion
mention	nation	potions	question	sections	station

1. **Florida** is to **state** as **Canada** is to _____

2. *All About Cats* is to **nonfiction** as *Pete the Cat* is to _____

3. **book** is to **chapters** as **newspaper** is to _____

4. **0.25** is to **decimal** as $\frac{1}{4}$ is to _____

5. **offer** is to **tag sale** as **bid** is to _____

6. **court** is to **house** as **police** is to _____

7. **spray** is to **perfume** as **rub** is to _____

8. **ask about** is to **inquire** as **tell about** is to _____

9. **effect** is to **cause** as **reaction** is to _____

10. **book jacket** is to **blurb** as **photograph** is to _____

UNIT 36

ng and *nk* Patterns

Focus

This week's focus is on *ng* and *nk* patterns in two-syllable words.

Helpful Hint

Notice that the hard *g* is vocalized when you add a suffix to words such as *long* (*longer*, *longest*) and *strong* (*stronger*, *strongest*). However, it is not vocalized when you add a suffix to other words such as *hang* (*hanger*, *hanging*) or *sing* (*singer*, *singing*).

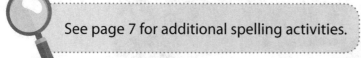
See page 7 for additional spelling activities.

➤ among
➤ angle
➤ angry
➤ ankle
➤ belong
➤ finger
➤ hanger
➤ hungry
➤ longest
➤ pinkish
➤ single
➤ sprinkle
➤ stronger
➤ wrinkle
➤ young

Sentence Completions

Name: _____ **Date:** _____

Directions: Use a word from the Word Bank to complete each sentence.

Word Bank					
among	ankle	belong	finger	hanger	hungry
longest	pinkish	single	sprinkle	wrinkled	young

1. John looks so tall when he stands _____ his classmates!

2. We need to iron your shirt because it got _____ .

3. Would you like to _____ some cinnamon on your applesauce?

4. There's some leftover chicken in the fridge if you're _____ .

5. Do you _____ to any teams or clubs?

6. The _____ car trip we've ever taken is seven hours.

7. I twisted my _____ when I was running to catch the bus.

8. Look how _____ Dad looks in that picture. I barely recognize him!

9. My sister broke up with her boyfriend, so now she's _____ .

10. It looks like I missed a _____ when I painted my nails.

Name: _____ **Date:** _____

Directions: Use a word from the Word Bank to complete each section.

Word Bank					
among	angles	angry	finger	hanger	hungry
longest	pinkish	single	stronger	wrinkle	young

Write a synonym for each word.

1. with _____

2. one _____

3. furious _____

4. digit _____

Write an antonym for each word.

5. old _____

6. shortest _____

7. weaker _____

8. full _____

Write a word that fits each category.

9. parallel lines, sides, curves, _____

10. crease, pleat, furrow, _____

11. reddish, yellowish, bluish, _____

12. hook, clip, clothespin, _____

Synonyms and Antonyms

Prefixes and Suffixes

Name: _____ **Date:** _____

Directions: The suffix –*er* means *more,* and the suffix –*est* means *most.* Add the suffixes –*er* and –*est* to each word to create new words. Double the consonant as needed.

1. young _____ _____

2. long _____ _____

3. strong _____ _____

4. big _____ _____

5. dark _____ _____

6. smart _____ _____

7. old _____ _____

8. neat _____ _____

9. wet _____ _____

10. safe _____ _____

Directions: Choose a word from your answers above to complete each sentence.

11. Please use your _____ handwriting when you make Grammy's card.

12. My baby sister is six years _____ than I am.

13. The _____ place to go during a tornado is in the basement.

14. Rosa is the _____ person here, so she gets to carry the heaviest box!

Name: _____ **Date:**_____

Directions: Sort the words in the Word Bank into two categories: *Adjectives* and *Nouns*. Write each word in the correct column.

Word Bank				
angry	pinkish	hanger	stronger	ankle
young	wrinkles	finger	angle	hungry

Adjectives	Nouns
◯	◯
◯	◯
◯	◯
◯	◯
◯	◯

Directions: Write all 10 words in ABC order.

1. _____   6. _____

2. _____   7. _____

3. _____   8. _____

4. _____   9. _____

5. _____   10. _____

Analogies

Name: _____ **Date:** _____

Directions: Use a word from the Word Bank to complete each analogy.

Word Bank					
angry	ankle	fingers	hanger	hungry	longest
pinkish	single	sprinkle	stronger	wrinkles	young

1. **stain remover** is to **stains** as **iron** is to _____

2. **second base** is to **double** as **first base** is to _____

3. **foot** is to **toes** as **hand** is to _____

4. **backpack** is to **hook** as **coat** is to _____

5. **drink** is to **thirsty** as **eat** is to _____

6. **milk** is to **pour** as **sugar** is to _____

7. **open arms** is to **happy** as **crossed arms** is to _____

8. **sick** is to **greenish** as **embarrassed** is to _____

9. **Mount Everest** is to **tallest** as **Nile River** is to _____

10. **bracelet** is to **wrist** as **anklet** is to _____

Answer Key

Week 1 Day 1 (page 12)

1. sample
2. fabric
3. handle
4. glasses
5. candle
6. taxes
7. plastic
8. traffic
9. paddle
10. apple

Week 1 Day 2 (page 13)

1. fabric
2. battle
3. paddle
4. handle
5. attic
6. sample
7. classic
8. vanish
9. apple
10. saddle
11. plastic
12. candle

Week 1 Day 3 (page 14)

Responses should be phrased as the correct sentence types.

Week 1 Day 4 (page 15)

1. taxes, taxing, taxed
2. paddles, paddling, paddled
3. samples, sampling, sampled
4. battleship, battles, battlefield
5. handlebars, handles, handled
6. candles, candlestick, candlelight
7. vanishes, vanishing, vanished

Week 1 Day 5 (page 16)

1. glasses
2. paddle
3. apple
4. traffic
5. fabric
6. handle
7. classic
8. candle
9. saddle
10. taxes

Week 2 Day 1 (page 18)

1. middle
2. finish
3. scribble
4. build
5. sizzle
6. little
7. griddle
8. kisses
9. simple
10. dishes

Week 2 Day 2 (page 19)

1. middle
2. wiggle
3. simple
4. mixes
5. finish
6. brittle
7. little
8. build
9. dishes
10. giggle
11. sizzle
12. kisses

Week 2 Day 3 (page 20)

1. misspell
2. mistake
3. misplaced
4. misbehave
5. miscounted
6. misprint
7. mistreat
8. mismatched
9. mislabel
10. misunderstand
11. miscounted
12. mistreat
13. misplaced
14. misspell
15. mistake
16. mismatched

Week 2 Day 4 (page 21)

1. mixes, mixing, mixed
2. kisses, kissing, kissed
3. finishes, finishing, finished
4. built, builder, building
5. simplest, simply, simplify
6. giggly, giggles, giggling
7. dishwasher, dishes, dishcloth

Week 2 Day 5 (page 22)

1. wiggle
2. sizzle
3. kisses
4. build
5. giggle
6. mixes
7. little
8. middle
9. scribble
10. finish

Week 3 Day 1 (page 24)

1. weather
2. heavy
3. dresses
4. breath
5. health
6. medic
7. ready
8. pebble
9. relish
10. spread

Week 3 Day 2 (page 25)

1. health
2. ready
3. meddle
4. settle
5. heavy
6. pebble
7. spread
8. selfish
9. relish
10. dresses
11. thread
12. bread

Week 3 Day 3 (page 26)

Responses should be phrased as the correct sentence types.

Week 3 Day 4 (page 27)

1. threads, threading, threaded
2. dresses, dressing, dressed
3. meddles, meddling, meddled
4. breathless, breathes, breathing
5. settled, settlement, settler
6. widespread, bedspread, spreading
7. heaviest, heavier, heavily

Week 3 Day 5 (page 28)

1. bread
2. thread
3. heavy
4. dresses
5. weather
6. breath
7. pebble
8. settle
9. medic
10. selfish

Week 4 Day 1 (page 30)

1. topple
2. bottle
3. foxes
4. gobble
5. tropics
6. polish
7. comic
8. hobble
9. boxes
10. topic

Week 4 Day 2 (page 31)

1. comic
2. polish
3. hobble
4. nozzle
5. toxic
6. wobble
7. gobble
8. topple
9. bottle
10. boxes
11. foxes
12. goggles

Week 4 Day 3 (page 32)

1. nonfiction
2. nonfat
3. nonstop
4. nonslip
5. nonstick
6. nonviolent
7. nonsense
8. nonprofit
9. nonrefundable
10. nonperishable
11. nonfat
12. nonfiction
13. nonslip
14. nonstop
15. nonstick
16. nonperishable

Answer Key (cont.)

Week 4 Day 4 (page 33)

Nouns: bottle, comic, foxes, goggles, nozzle
Verbs: gobble, hobble, polished, topple, wobble
ABC Order: bottle, comic, foxes, gobble, goggles, hobble, nozzle, polished, topple, wobble

Week 4 Day 5 (page 34)

1. optic
2. polish
3. goggles
4. bottle
5. nozzle
6. wobble
7. gobble
8. toxic
9. boxes
10. hobble

Week 5 Day 1 (page 36)

1. double
2. money
3. front
4. puzzle
5. country
6. touch
7. cover
8. punish
9. month
10. public

Week 5 Day 2 (page 37)

1. country
2. touch
3. couple
4. money
5. front
6. public
7. punish
8. trouble
9. jungle
10. double
11. month
12. cover

Week 5 Day 3 (page 38)

Responses should be phrased as the correct sentence types.

Week 5 Day 4 (page 39)

1. covers, covering, covered
2. puzzles, puzzling, puzzled
3. troubles, troubling, troubled
4. published, publication, publisher
5. untouched, touches, touching
6. beachfront, forefront, frontline
7. bubbly, bubblegum, bubbles

Week 5 Day 5 (page 40)

1. jungle
2. public
3. country
4. bubble
5. puzzle
6. month
7. touch
8. double
9. money
10. publish

Week 6 Day 1 (page 42)

1. jockeys
2. tackle
3. freckles
4. nickels
5. jacket
6. bucket
7. rockets
8. chuckle
9. crackle
10. socket

Week 6 Day 2 (page 43)

1. unlucky
2. unsteady
3. unbuckle
4. unzip
5. unlock
6. uncover
7. unwrap
8. unplug
9. unhelpful
10. unpack
11. unzip
12. unpack
13. unplug
14. unwrap
15. unlock
16. unsteady

Week 6 Day 3 (page 44)

Nouns: pickle, jockey, jacket, nickel, bucket
Verbs: pocketed, buckled, tackle, crackle, chuckle
ABC Order: bucket, buckled, chuckle, crackle, jacket, jockey, nickel, pickle, pocketed, tackle

Week 6 Day 4 (page 45)

1. chuckles, chuckling, chuckled
2. tickets, ticketing, ticketed
3. tackles, tackling, tackled
4. pockets, pocketbook, pocketful
5. crackled, crackling, crackly
6. dill pickle, pickled, pickling
7. skyrocket, rocketed, rockets

Week 6 Day 5 (page 46)

1. hockey
2. jockey
3. pickle
4. nickel
5. buckle
6. bucket
7. ticket
8. crackle
9. jacket
10. chuckle

Week 7 Day 1 (page 48)

1. knuckle
2. assigns
3. resign
4. sign
5. bristles
6. hustle
7. nestle
8. castle
9. design
10. rustle

Week 7 Day 2 (page 49)

1. castle
2. nestle
3. design
4. wrestle
5. assign
6. climb
7. hustle
8. resign
9. knuckle
10. wriggle
11. bristle
12. whistle

Week 7 Day 3 (page 50)

Responses should be phrased as the correct sentence types.

Week 7 Day 4 (page 51)

1. assigns, assigning, assigned
2. bustles, bustling, bustled
3. wrestles, wrestling, wrestled
4. designer, designs, designed
5. climbed, climbing, climber
6. knuckleball, knucklehead, knuckles
7. signed, signature, signal

Week 7 Day 5 (page 52)

1. bristle
2. whistle
3. castle
4. resign
5. rustle
6. climb
7. knuckle
8. wrestle
9. wriggle
10. design

Week 8 Day 1 (page 54)

1. explode
2. promote
3. paste
4. exhales
5. waste
6. excuse
7. decade
8. propose
9. refuse
10. delete

Week 8 Day 2 (page 55)

1. mistake
2. paste
3. explode
4. delete
5. exhale
6. include
7. waste
8. refuse
9. taste
10. excuse
11. decade
12. provide

Answer Key (cont.)

Week 8 Day 3 (page 56)

1. infield
2. indoors
3. inmates
4. inside
5. inhale
6. income
7. indent
8. inject
9. intake
10. ingrown
11. inside
12. ingrown
13. income
14. inmates
15. inhale
16. inject

Week 8 Day 4 (page 57)

1. exhales, exhaling, exhaled
2. excuses, excusing, excused
3. deletes, deleting, deleted
4. tasteful, tasty, taste buds
5. wasteful, wasted, wasting
6. proposal, proposing, proposed
7. explosion, exploded, explosive

Week 8 Day 5 (page 58)

1. exhale
2. taste
3. delete
4. invite
5. decade
6. promote
7. explode
8. propose
9. paste
10. include

Week 9 Day 1 (page 60)

1. glance
2. fence
3. since
4. decide
5. fancy
6. produce
7. recite
8. once
9. excite
10. precise

Week 9 Day 2 (page 61)

1. glance
2. chance
3. produce
4. device
5. fancy
6. precise
7. reduce
8. excite
9. fence
10. once
11. dance
12. prince

Week 9 Day 3 (page 62)

Soft c Words: fancy, fence, dance, recite, once, precise, decide, prince, since, reduce
Hard c Words: across, because, cattle, couple, compete, classes, cried, cuddle, excuse, include
Pattern: Hard c comes before a, o, u, l, and r. Soft c comes before e, i, and y.

Week 9 Day 4 (page 63)

1. glances, glancing, glanced
2. excites, exciting, excited
3. reduces, reducing, reduced
4. decided, deciding, decision
5. dancer, danced, dancing
6. productive, producer, product
7. precisely, imprecise, precision

Week 9 Day 5 (page 64)

1. once
2. prince
3. dance
4. fancy
5. fence
6. device
7. produce
8. recite
9. excite
10. decide

Week 10 Day 1 (page 66)

1. sponge
2. guests
3. tragic
4. trudged
5. plunge
6. bridge
7. guilty
8. change
9. guide
10. pledge

Week 10 Day 2 (page 67)

1. pledge
2. plunge
3. cringe
4. guide
5. guilty
6. gentle
7. guest
8. change
9. judge
10. trudge
11. magic
12. sponge

Week 10 Day 3 (page 68)

Soft g Words: bridge, gym, judge, magic, pledge, plunge, pudgy, sponge, tragic, trudge
Hard g Words: angle, gather, glossy, gobble, grass, griddle, guess, guest, guide, guilty
Pattern: Hard g comes before a, o, u, l, and r. Soft g comes before e, i, and y.

Week 10 Day 4 (page 69)

1. trudges, trudging, trudged
2. pledges, pledging, pledged
3. changes, changing, changed
4. magical, magically, magician
5. guiding, guidance, guided
6. spongy, sponging, sponges
7. plunging, plunged, plunger

Week 10 Day 5 (page 70)

1. sponge
2. judge
3. bridge
4. guest
5. guy
6. cringe
7. plunge
8. guide
9. guilty
10. trudge

Week 11 Day 1 (page 72)

1. trophy
2. enough
3. crutches
4. scratch
5. stretch
6. catch
7. phonics
8. tough
9. snatch
10. stitches

Week 11 Day 2 (page 73)

1. snatch
2. laugh
3. scratch
4. graphics
5. rough
6. tough
7. stretch
8. catch
9. sketch
10. enough
11. trophy
12. witch

Week 11 Day 3 (page 74)

Singular Nouns: witch, trophy, watch, phone, kitchen
Plural Nouns: matches, stitches, crutches, patches, photos
ABC Order: crutches, kitchen, matches, patches, phone, photos, stitches, trophy, watch, witch

Week 11 Day 4 (page 75)

1. scratches, scratching, scratched
2. stretches, stretching, stretched
3. stitches, stitching, stitched
4. caught, catching, catcher
5. laughter, laughing, laughed
6. tougher, toughen, toughest
7. roughly, roughest, rougher

Answer Key (cont.)

Week 11 Day 5 (page 76)

1. phonics
2. rough
3. stitches
4. crutches
5. witch
6. catch
7. trophy
8. scratch
9. sketch
10. graphics

Week 12 Day 1 (page 78)

1. fable
2. table
3. gravy
4. lazy
5. staple
6. lady
7. paper
8. ladle
9. baby
10. stable

Week 12 Day 2 (page 79)

1. baby
2. lady
3. craters
4. ladle
5. lazy
6. basic
7. later
8. crazy
9. staple
10. stable
11. fable
12. gravy

Week 12 Day 3 (page 80)

Nouns: gravy, lady, paper, baby, table
Adjectives: crazy, lazy, basic, able, hazy
ABC Order: able, baby, basic, crazy, gravy, hazy, lady, lazy, paper, table

Week 12 Day 4 (page 81)

Answers should include the bold spelling words.

Week 12 Day 5 (page 82)

1. gravy
2. table
3. lady
4. baby
5. fable
6. stable
7. ladle
8. paper
9. basic
10. later

Week 13 Day 1 (page 84)

1. freight
2. explain
3. exclaim
4. delay
5. details
6. veins
7. afraid
8. sleighs
9. veil
10. betray

Week 13 Day 2 (page 85)

1. exclude
2. exit
3. export
4. explain
5. exclaim
6. expire
7. extinct
8. expel
9. exhale
10. extend
11. exhale
12. exclude
13. exclaim
14. extend
15. exit
16. expel

Week 13 Day 3 (page 86)

Nouns: sleigh, crayons, veil, veins, freight
Verbs: exclaim, explain, weigh, delay, raise
ABC Order: crayons, delay, exclaim, explain, freight, raise, sleigh, veil, veins, weigh

Week 13 Day 4 (page 87)

Answers should include the bold spelling words.

Week 13 Day 5 (page 88)

1. holiday
2. veil
3. eight
4. freight
5. raise
6. veins
7. weigh
8. praise
9. exclaim
10. sleigh

Week 14 Day 1 (page 90)

1. squeeze
2. breathe
3. cheese
4. grease
5. peace
6. freeze
7. creases
8. lease
9. sneeze
10. leave

Week 14 Day 2 (page 91)

1. breathe
2. grease
3. squeeze
4. breeze
5. peace
6. freeze
7. leave
8. weave
9. cheese
10. sneeze
11. please
12. crease

Week 14 Day 3 (page 92)

1. squeezes, squeezing, squeezed sneezes, sneezing, sneezed
2. breathes, breathing, breathed
3. frozen, freezing, freezer
4. leaving, left, leaves
5. cheeseburger, cheesecake, cheesy
6. pleasing, pleasure, pleasant

Week 14 Day 4 (page 93)

Answers should include the bold spelling words.

Week 14 Day 5 (page 94)

1. sleeve
2. weave
3. breeze
4. freeze
5. breathe
6. cheese
7. wheeze
8. sneeze
9. lease
10. leave

Week 15 Day 1 (page 96)

1. people
2. ceiling
3. easy
4. receive
5. eagle
6. steeple
7. deceive
8. beneath
9. agree
10. asleep

Week 15 Day 2 (page 97)

1. people
2. weird
3. steeple
4. deceive
5. receive
6. easy
7. asleep
8. ceiling
9. eagle
10. beetle
11. between
12. needle

Week 15 Day 3 (page 98)

1. fearless
2. cheerful
3. sleeveless
4. tearful
5. sleepless
6. speechless
7. peaceful
8. useless
9. graceful
10. careful
11. sleeveless
12. peaceful
13. tearful
14. speechless
15. graceful
16. useless

Answer Key (cont.)

Week 15 Day 4 (page 99)

Answers should include the bold spelling words.

Week 15 Day 5 (page 100)

1. needle
2. agree
3. asleep
4. people
5. ceiling
6. eagle
7. either
8. receive
9. beetle
10. between

Week 16 Day 1 (page 102)

1. lightning
2. apply
3. spider
4. title
5. buy
6. deny
7. tiger
8. reply
9. dial
10. trial

Week 16 Day 2 (page 103)

1. reply
2. icy
3. buy
4. rely
5. deny
6. dial
7. slimy
8. supply
9. July
10. trial
11. title
12. tiger

Week 16 Day 3 (page 104)

1. supplies, supplying, supplied
2. relies, relying, relied
3. frightens, frightening, frightened
4. buying, bought, buys
5. denied, denial, denying
6. icing, iced, ice rink
7. lighten, lightness, light

Week 16 Day 4 (page 105)

1. shyness
2. tightness
3. dryness
4. blindness
5. kindness
6. illness
7. freshness
8. weakness
9. darkness
10. thickness
11. darkness
12. blindness
13. illness
14. shyness
15. dryness
16. kindness

Week 16 Day 5 (page 106)

1. tiger
2. title
3. buy
4. lightning
5. spider
6. slimy
7. deny
8. rely
9. apply
10. dial

Week 17 Day 1 (page 108)

1. bowl
2. pillow
3. window
4. hollow
5. follow
6. yellow
7. meadow
8. mellow
9. grown
10. shallow

Week 17 Day 2 (page 109)

1. meadow
2. shadow
3. below
4. pillow
5. hollow
6. follow
7. mellow
8. shallow
9. elbow
10. yellow
11. bowl
12. widow

Week 17 Day 3 (page 110)

Adjectives: yellow, hollow, mellow, shallow, narrow
Nouns: pillow, window, widow, bowl, meadow
ABC Order: bowl, hollow, meadow, mellow, narrow, pillow, shallow, widow, window, yellow

Week 17 Day 4 (page 111)

Answers should include the bold spelling words.

Week 17 Day 5 (page 112)

1. bowl
2. elbow
3. window
4. yellow
5. pillow
6. rainbow
7. meadow
8. shallow
9. below
10. grown

Week 18 Day 1 (page 114)

1. program
2. though
3. dough
4. hotel
5. smoky
6. shoulder
7. ghost
8. toll
9. poll
10. scroll

Week 18 Day 2 (page 115)

1. poll
2. toll
3. noble
4. program
5. bony
6. smoky
7. stroll
8. boulder
9. hotel
10. shoulder
11. ghost
12. dough

Week 18 Day 3 (page 116)

1. pole
2. roll
3. doe
4. close
5. grown
6. role
7. shown
8. dough
9. groan
10. shone

Week 18 Day 4 (page 117)

1. polls, polling, polled
2. follows, following, followed
3. boasts, boasting, boasted
4. smoke, smoking, smokehouse
5. bone, bone-chilling, backbone
6. stroller, strolled, strolling
7. doughy, doughnut, doughboy

Week 18 Day 5 (page 118)

1. dough
2. shoulders
3. robot
4. stroll
5. hotel
6. boulder
7. program
8. smoky
9. toll
10. scroll

Week 19 Day 1 (page 120)

1. route
2. cruise
3. through
4. choose
5. loose
6. truth
7. juice
8. move
9. soup
10. lose

Week 19 Day 2 (page 121)

1. cruise
2. fuel
3. choose
4. cruel
5. loose
6. truth
7. lose
8. move
9. bruise
10. soup
11. through
12. juice

Answer Key *(cont.)*

Week 19 Day 3 (page 122)

1. threw
2. chews
3. roots
4. too
5. choose
6. through
7. to
8. flew
9. two
10. flu

Week 19 Day 4 (page 123)

Answers should include the bold spelling words.

Week 19 Day 5 (page 124)

1. soup
2. cruise
3. prove
4. lose
5. loose
6. group
7. fuel
8. through
9. move
10. cruel

Week 20 Day 1 (page 126)

1. balloon
2. music
3. recruit
4. value
5. shampoo
6. cartoons
7. remove
8. argue
9. rescue
10. duty

Week 20 Day 2 (page 127)

1. value
2. rescue
3. pursue
4. duty
5. remove
6. improve
7. nephew
8. recruit
9. balloons
10. music
11. shampoo
12. bugle

Week 20 Day 3 (page 128)

Verbs: pursue, improve, remove, rescue, argue
Nouns: noodle, balloon, shampoo, cartoon, bugle
ABC Order: argue, balloon, bugle, cartoon, improve, noodle, pursue, remove, rescue, shampoo

Week 20 Day 4 (page 129)

1. removes, removing, removed
2. pursues, pursuing, pursued
3. bruises, bruising, bruised
4. improvement, improving, improved
5. argument, argued, arguing
6. duties, off-duty, heavy-duty
7. valued, valuable, undervalued

Week 20 Day 5 (page 130)

1. balloon
2. music
3. shampoo
4. rescue
5. nephew
6. noodles
7. bugle
8. argue
9. cartoon
10. recruit

Week 21 Day 1 (page 132)

1. compete
2. complete
3. contain
4. collide
5. should've
6. convince
7. combine
8. could've
9. collapse
10. results

Week 21 Day 2 (page 133)

1. pulse
2. convince
3. combine
4. result
5. insult
6. complete
7. bulge
8. contrast
9. collapse
10. should've
11. compete
12. contain

Week 21 Day 3 (page 134)

1. contain
2. collide
3. convince
4. contrast
5. combine
6. compete
7. contract
8. compare
9. compose
10. collapse
11. collide
12. compete
13. compare
14. contain
15. combine
16. contract

Week 21 Day 4 (page 135)

Answers should include the bold spelling words.

Week 21 Day 5 (page 136)

1. pulse
2. should've
3. compete
4. bulge
5. contain
6. contrast
7. complete
8. collapse
9. control
10. insult

Week 22 Day 1 (page 138)

1. scrounged
2. devoured
3. chowder
4. discount
5. hourly
6. amount
7. spouses
8. shower
9. blouse
10. mouse

Week 22 Day 2 (page 139)

1. bounce
2. pounce
3. house
4. spouse
5. drowsy
6. allow
7. devour
8. discount
9. chowder
10. hourly
11. blouse
12. scrounge

Week 22 Day 3 (page 140)

1. underfed
2. underpaid
3. undercover
4. underground
5. underpass
6. underwater
7. underwear
8. underfoot
9. understand
10. undergo
11. underwater
12. underfed
13. undergo
14. underwear
15. understand
16. underground

Week 22 Day 4 (page 141)

1. bounces, bouncing, bounced
2. scrounges, scrounging, scrounged
3. discounts, discounting, discounted
4. houses, lighthouse, outhouse
5. allowed, allowance, allowing
6. hour, hours, hourglass
7. drowsier, drowsily, drowsiness

Week 22 Day 5 (page 142)

1. blouse
2. shower
3. spouse
4. devour
5. mouse
6. pounce
7. drowsy
8. hourly
9. house
10. amount

Week 23 Day 1 (page 144)

1. employ
2. destroy
3. appoint
4. loiter
5. avoid
6. noise
7. rejoiced
8. foyer
9. annoy
10. oily

Answer Key (cont.)

Week 23 Day 2 (page 145)

1.	employ	7.	destroy
2.	deploy	8.	joyful
3.	choice	9.	annoy
4.	rejoice	10.	foyer
5.	noise	11.	loiter
6.	enjoy	12.	oily

Week 23 Day 3 (page 146)

1. employs, employing, employed
2. avoids, avoiding, avoided
3. appoints, appointing, appointed
4. choose, chosen, choices
5. voices, voicemail, vocal
6. noisy, noises, noisemaker
7. enjoy, joy, joyous

Week 23 Day 4 (page 147)

Answers should include the bold spelling words.

Week 23 Day 5 (page 148)

1.	voices	6.	deploy
2.	noise	7.	choice
3.	appoint	8.	destroy
4.	foyer	9.	employ
5.	loiter	10.	annoying

Week 24 Day 1 (page 150)

1.	pause	6.	autumn
2.	waffle	7.	sauce
3.	laundry	8.	water
4.	swallow	9.	caught
5.	naughty	10.	taught

Week 24 Day 2 (page 151)

1.	launch	7.	daughter
2.	autumn	8.	naughty
3.	swallow	9.	sauce
4.	pause	10.	gauze
5.	false	11.	water
6.	cause	12.	laundry

Week 24 Day 3 (page 152)

1. causes, causing, caused
2. swallows, swallowing, swallowed
3. haunts, haunting, haunted
4. teacher, teaches, teach
5. catcher, catches, catch
6. saucy, applesauce, saucepan
7. waterfall, watery, saltwater

Week 24 Day 4 (page 153)

1.	preheat	9.	prescribe
2.	preschool	10.	pretaught
3.	prepay	11.	predict
4.	preteen	12.	preteen
5.	predict	13.	preview
6.	prefix	14.	precaution
7.	precaution	15.	prepay
8.	preview	16.	preheat

Week 24 Day 5 (page 154)

1.	daughter	6.	gauze
2.	taught	7.	cause
3.	waffles	8.	swallow
4.	saucer	9.	launch
5.	water	10.	autumn

Week 25 Day 1 (page 156)

1.	fought	6.	often
2.	brought	7.	lacrosse
3.	broad	8.	bought
4.	across	9.	ought
5.	frolic	10.	offer

Week 25 Day 2 (page 157)

1.	frolic	7.	ought
2.	thought	8.	broad
3.	bossy	9.	trough
4.	bought	10.	cough
5.	frosty	11.	lacrosse
6.	offer	12.	often

Week 25 Day 3 (page 158)

Past Tense Verbs: bought, brought, fought, thought, caught
Present Tense Verbs: buy, catch, bring, think, fight
ABC Order: bought, bring, brought, buy, catch, caught, fight, fought, think, thought

Week 25 Day 4 (page 159)

1.	taught	6.	clause
2.	haul	7.	cause
3.	bawl	8.	claws
4.	paws	9.	pause
5.	alter	10.	hall

Week 25 Day 5 (page 160)

1.	Frosty	6.	brought
2.	cough	7.	thought
3.	trough	8.	bossy
4.	lacrosse	9.	bought
5.	broad	10.	across

Week 26 Day 1 (page 162)

1.	hearts	6.	tardy
2.	sparkle	7.	hardly
3.	garlic	8.	remark
4.	large	9.	guard
5.	party	10.	garnish

Week 26 Day 2 (page 163)

1.	hardly	7.	sparkle
2.	guard	8.	large
3.	garnish	9.	army
4.	remark	10.	heart
5.	tardy	11.	artist
6.	farther	12.	garlic

Week 26 Day 3 (page 164)

1.	darken	9.	widen
2.	sharpen	10.	brighten
3.	harden	11.	sharpen
4.	soften	12.	darken
5.	loosen	13.	brighten
6.	freshen	14.	tighten
7.	tighten	15.	soften
8.	ripen	16.	ripen

Week 26 Day 4 (page 165)

Answers should include the bold spelling words.

Week 26 Day 5 (page 166)

1.	army	6.	large
2.	party	7.	partner
3.	sparkle	8.	marbles
4.	heart	9.	garlic
5.	artist	10.	remark

Answer Key (cont.)

Week 27 Day 1 (page 168)

1.	prepare	6.	pare
2.	barely	7.	squares
3.	aware	8.	spare
4.	Beware	9.	share
5.	careful	10.	fare

Week 27 Day 2 (page 169)

1.	prepare	7.	careful
2.	declare	8.	aware
3.	spare	9.	square
4.	barely	10.	fare
5.	rare	11.	pare
6.	glare	12.	stare

Week 27 Day 3 (page 170)

1. shares, sharing, shared
2. prepares, preparing, prepared
3. declares, declaring, declared
4. care, careless, caretaker
5. bare, barefoot, threadbare
6. farewell, bus fare, airfare
7. scare, scared, scarecrow

Week 27 Day 4 (page 171)

Verbs: glare, prepare, stare, declare, share
Adjectives: rare, square, scary, careful, aware
ABC Order: aware, careful, declare, glare, prepare, rare, scary, share, square, stare

Week 27 Day 5 (page 172)

1.	glare	6.	rare
2.	scary	7.	prepare
3.	barely	8.	spare
4.	stare	9.	fare
5.	square	10.	beware

Week 28 Day 1 (page 174)

1.	swear	6.	airplane
2.	dairy	7.	prairie
3.	despair	8.	repair
4.	pears	9.	fairy
5.	impair	10.	tear

Week 28 Day 2 (page 175)

1.	prairie	7.	despair
2.	fairy	8.	impair
3.	swear	9.	pear
4.	wear	10.	bear
5.	repair	11.	dairy
6.	tear	12.	wheelchair

Week 28 Day 3 (page 176)

1. swears, swearing, swore
   wears, wearing, wore
2. impairs, impairing, impaired
   repairs, repairing, repaired
3. chairlift, chair, chairman
4. repairable, repairman, disrepair
5. stairwell, stair, downstairs
6. air, airline, airbag

Week 28 Day 4 (page 177)

1.	bear	6.	stares
2.	fare	7.	fair
3.	wear	8.	pair
4.	bare	9.	pear
5.	hare	10.	hair

Week 28 Day 5 (page 178)

1.	dairy	6.	airplane
2.	fairy	7.	bear
3.	wear	8.	fairground
4.	pears	9.	repair
5.	wheelchair	10.	prairie

Week 29 Day 1 (page 180)

1.	morning	6.	stormy
2.	acorns	7.	report
3.	record	8.	order
4.	transport	9.	perform
5.	reform	10.	border

Week 29 Day 2 (page 181)

1.	transport	7.	morning
2.	story	8.	record
3.	border	9.	stormy
4.	reform	10.	acorns
5.	northern	11.	popcorn
6.	import	12.	forty

Week 29 Day 3 (page 182)

1.	reform	9.	resend
2.	report	10.	reenter
3.	record	11.	rebuild
4.	retell	12.	refill
5.	rebuild	13.	resend
6.	refill	14.	record
7.	refinish	15.	retell
8.	react	16.	report

Week 29 Day 4 (page 183)

Answers should include the bold spelling words.

Week 29 Day 5 (page 184)

1.	morning	6.	record
2.	stormy	7.	story
3.	northern	8.	perform
4.	acorns	9.	transport
5.	borders	10.	forty

Week 30 Day 1 (page 186)

1.	course	6.	board
2.	ignore	7.	court
3.	source	8.	poor
4.	floor	9.	soar
5.	horse	10.	door

Week 30 Day 2 (page 187)

1.	soar	7.	floor
2.	explore	8.	divorce
3.	force	9.	horse
4.	roar	10.	door
5.	poor	11.	board
6.	ignore	12.	court

Week 30 Day 3 (page 188)

1. explores, exploring, explored
   ignores, ignoring, ignored
2. enforces, enforcing, enforced
   divorces, divorcing, divorced
3. cardboard, chalkboard, whiteboard
4. courthouse, courtroom, courts
5. doorknob, doorbell, doorway
6. horseshoe, seahorse, racehorse

Answer Key (cont.)

Week 30 Day 4 (page 189)

1. sore
2. pour
3. soar
4. poor
5. horse
6. coarse
7. hoarse
8. board
9. four
10. for

Week 30 Day 5 (page 190)

1. floor
2. roar
3. court
4. horse
5. door
6. divorce
7. poor
8. explore
9. soar
10. course

Week 31 Day 1 (page 192)

1. warm
2. worth
3. world
4. worry
5. ward
6. quarter
7. worst
8. worthless
9. quart
10. worse

Week 31 Day 2 (page 193)

1. world
2. worth
3. warn
4. worst
5. war
6. work
7. warm
8. worse
9. quarter
10. wart
11. ward
12. worm

Week 31 Day 3 (page 194)

1. intercom
2. interrupt
3. interstate
4. interview
5. intercept
6. intermission
7. interfere
8. international
9. intersection
10. interpret
11. intermission
12. international
13. interstate
14. intercom
15. intersection

Week 31 Day 4 (page 195)

Answers should include the bold spelling words.

Week 31 Day 5 (page 196)

1. worm
2. war
3. warm
4. worry
5. work
6. worst
7. quart
8. world
9. wards
10. warts

Week 32 Day 1 (page 198)

1. pattern
2. desert
3. alert
4. merge
5. swerve
6. verse
7. danger
8. prefer
9. reverse
10. serve

Week 32 Day 2 (page 199)

1. alert
2. merge
3. pattern
4. prefer
5. reverse
6. danger
7. every
8. never
9. desert
10. nerves
11. verse
12. stranger

Week 32 Day 3 (page 200)

1. overdo
2. overdue
3. overhead
4. overreacts
5. overtime
6. overdose
7. oversleep
8. overcooked
9. overweight
10. overcharged
11. oversleep
12. overtime
13. overcharged
14. overcooked
15. overhead
16. overdue

Week 32 Day 4 (page 201)

1. prefers, preferring, preferred
2. serves, serving, served
3. alerts, alerting, alerted
4. dangerous, dangers, endanger
5. reversal, reversed, reversing
6. strange, strangely, strangest
7. merging, merged, merges

Week 32 Day 5 (page 202)

1. desert
2. verse
3. pattern
4. serve
5. reverse
6. nerves
7. stranger
8. alert
9. germs
10. every

Week 33 Day 1 (page 204)

1. surprise
2. nurse
3. during
4. hurry
5. purple
6. pure
7. disturb
8. curse
9. cures
10. purse

Week 33 Day 2 (page 205)

1. hurry
2. cure
3. disturb
4. urge
5. sturdy
6. curse
7. blurry
8. pure
9. purse
10. purple
11. during
12. turtle

Week 33 Day 3 (page 206)

Adjectives: sturdy, blurry, purple, pure, curvy
Verbs: urge, cure, surprise, curse, disturb
ABC Order: blurry, cure, curse, curvy, disturb, pure, purple, sturdy, surprise, urge

Week 33 Day 4 (page 207)

Answers should include the bold spelling words.

Week 33 Day 5 (page 208)

1. purse
2. nurse
3. purple
4. turtle
5. curves
6. sturdy
7. disturb
8. surprised
9. cure
10. pure

Week 34 Day 1 (page 210)

1. search
2. dirty
3. pearl
4. heard
5. rehearse
6. Earth
7. thirsty
8. yearn
9. circle
10. learn

Answer Key (cont.)

Week 34 Day 2 (page 211)

1. search
2. earn
3. yearn
4. rehearse
5. early
6. firmly
7. dirty
8. learn
9. pearl
10. circle
11. Earth
12. thirty

Week 34 Day 3 (page 212)

1. learns, learning, learned
   earns, earning, earned
2. stirs, stirring, stirred
3. earthworm, earthquake, earthly
4. thirst, thirstier, thirstiest
5. earliest, earlier, early bird
6. rehearsal, rehearsing, rehearsed

Week 34 Day 4 (page 213)

1. heard
2. fir
3. birth
4. overdue
5. overdo
6. whir
7. fur
8. were
9. herd
10. oversees

Week 34 Day 5 (page 214)

1. heard
2. early
3. dirty
4. earn
5. birthday
6. circle
7. pearl
8. thirty
9. learn
10. thirsty

Week 35 Day 1 (page 216)

1. lotion
2. fiction
3. auction
4. nation
5. section
6. fraction
7. mention
8. option
9. station
10. caption

Week 35 Day 2 (page 217)

1. option
2. mention
3. motion
4. nation
5. fiction
6. question
7. section
8. caution
9. caption
10. lotion
11. potion
12. station

Week 35 Day 3 (page 218)

1. transport
2. transaction
3. transatlantic
4. transcontinental
5. transform
6. transplant
7. transform
8. translate
9. transparent
10. transmits
11. transcontinental
12. transport
13. transplant
14. transaction
15. transform
16. transparent

Week 35 Day 4 (page 219)

Answers should include the bold spelling words.

Week 35 Day 5 (page 220)

1. nation
2. fiction
3. sections
4. fraction
5. auction
6. station
7. lotion
8. mention
9. action
10. caption

Week 36 Day 1 (page 222)

1. among
2. wrinkled
3. sprinkle
4. hungry
5. belong
6. longest
7. ankle
8. young
9. single
10. finger

Week 36 Day 2 (page 223)

1. among
2. single
3. angry
4. finger
5. young
6. longest
7. stronger
8. hungry
9. angles
10. wrinkle
11. pinkish
12. hanger

Week 36 Day 3 (page 224)

1. younger, youngest
2. longer, longest
3. stronger, strongest
4. bigger, biggest
5. darker, darkest
6. smarter, smartest
7. older, oldest
8. neater, neatest
9. wetter, wettest
10. safer, safest
11. neatest
12. younger
13. safest
14. strongest

Week 36 Day 4 (page 225)

Adjectives: angry, pinkish, stronger, young, hungry
Nouns: hanger, ankle, wrinkles, finger, angle
ABC Order: angle, angry, ankle, finger, hanger, hungry, pinkish, stronger, wrinkles, young

Week 36 Day 5 (page 226)

1. wrinkles
2. single
3. fingers
4. hanger
5. hungry
6. sprinkle
7. angry
8. pinkish
9. longest
10. ankle

Unit Assessments

At the end of each unit, use the corresponding quiz to determine what students have learned. Ask students to spell the two words. Then, have students write the sentence. Say the words and sentence slowly, repeating as often as needed. The bolded words were studied in the unit.

Unit	Phonetic Pattern	Words	Sentence
1	short *a* words	babble, drastic	We found **candles** and **glasses** in Pam's **attic**.
2	short *i* words	fixes, thimble	My **little** sister **giggles** when she gives me **kisses**.
3	short *e* words	feather, kettle	Does the fabric make these **dresses** too **heavy** for warm **weather**?
4	short *o* words	cobble, politic	The stack of **boxes** started to **wobble** when I looked for my nail **polish**.
5	short *u* words	puddle, crumble	If you **touch** the **double bubble**, it will pop.
6	*ck* pattern	packet, trickle	Keep your **ticket** in your **pocket** until we get to the **hockey** game.
7	silent letters	thistle, cosign	When Mr. Grant blows his **whistle**, that's our **sign** to **hustle** and line up.
8	silent *e* words	expose, provoke	Jake **refused** to **taste** the free samples that the baker **provided**.
9	soft *c* words	France, incite	They've been making all kinds of **exciting devices** here **since** 2003.
10	soft and hard *g* words	smudge, hinge	You need to **change** the **sponge** before you **plunge** it into the soapy water.
11	consonant digraphs	batches, pitch	If you don't **stretch enough** before you run, you might end up on **crutches**.
12	long *a* words	shaky, cable	Please bring a **ladle** to the **table** so we can use it for the **gravy**.
13	long *a* vowel teams	remain, decay	Add more **details** to the part where you **explain** your ride on Santa's **sleigh**.
14	long *e* vowel teams	heave, teethe	**Please** don't wipe your nose on your **sleeve** after you **sneeze**.
15	more long *e* vowel teams	beagle, neither	Some **people** like to fall **asleep beneath** the stars.
16	long *i* vowel team and open syllables	imply, diner	We'll need to **buy** a large **supply** of paper goods for our party in **July**.
17	long *o* vowel team	willow, known	I looked out the **window** and saw a **rainbow** stretching over the **meadow**.
18	long *o* patterns	roll, rosy	Cody can **program** his **robot** to pick up heavy **boulders**.
19	long *u* patterns	goose, soothe	Don't forget to **choose** your **juice** when you **move through** the line.

Unit Assessments *(cont.)*

Unit	Phonetic Pattern	Words	Sentence
20	more long *u* patterns	poodle, ruby	My **nephew** got a **balloon** when he finished eating all his **noodles**.
21	schwa sound	compose, consult	The sandcastle **could've collapsed** when two kids **collided** near it.
22	*ou/ow* diphthongs	ounce, flower	If my cat sees a **mouse**, she will try to **pounce** and **devour** it.
23	*oi/oy* diphthongs	poise, boyish	I couldn't hear his **voice** because there was too much **noise** in the **foyer**.
24	*au/aw* digraphs	wander, staunch	Paul **taught** his **daughter** how to fold **laundry**.
25	/aw/ pattern with *ough* and *oa*	glossy, softer	I **thought** you **bought cough** drops at the store **across** the street.
26	*r*-controlled vowels with *ar*	barge, tarnish	An **artist** at the **party** painted **large hearts** and **sparkles** on our cheeks.
27	long *a* patterns with *are*	snare, barefoot	Be **careful** when you **prepare** apples with a **paring** knife.
28	long *a* patterns with *air* and *ear*	stairwell, underwear	Can you **repair** the **tear** in my jacket so I can **wear** it on the **airplane**?
29	*r*-controlled vowels with *or*	export, boring	We popped enough **popcorn** for **forty** people this **morning**.
30	*r*-controlled vowels with *oar*, *oor*, *our*, *ore*	yourself, doorbell	You can't **ignore** the fastest **horse** when he races around the **course**.
31	*r*-controlled vowels with *quar*, *war*, *wor*	warp, worthy	Having a **wart** on your thumb is not the **worst** thing in the **world**!
32	*r*-controlled vowels with *er*	refer, verge	Remember to stay **alert every** time you **merge** into traffic.
33	*r*-controlled vowels with *ur*	gurgle, purge	Are you sure the **nurse** keeps stickers in her **purple purse**?
34	*r*-controlled vowels with *ear* and *ir*	earl, squirmy	I **heard** that Mrs. Burns is turning **thirty** on her next **birthday**.
35	*–tion* ending	notion, equation	Read every **section** and all the **captions** before you look at the **questions**.
36	*ng* and *nk* patterns	clingy, twinkle	**Young** kids sat **among** the **hungry** ducks and fed them bread with their **fingers**.

Spelling Categories

Spelling Category	Spelling Pattern	Unit
Short Vowels	short *a* words	1
	short *i* words	2
	short *e* words	3
	short *o* words	4
	short *u* words	5
Consonant Digraphs and Blends	*ck* pattern	6
	consonant digraphs	11
	ng and *nk* patterns	36
Silent and Soft Letters	silent letters	7
	silent *e* words	8
	soft *c* words	9
	soft and hard *g* words	10
	–*tion* ending	35
Long Vowels	long *a* words	12
	long *a* vowel teams	13
	long *e* vowel teams	14
	more long *e* vowel teams	15
	long *i* vowel team and open syllables	16
	long *o* vowel team	17
	long *o* patterns	18
	long *u* patterns	19
	more long *u* patterns	20
Ambiguous Vowels	schwa sound	21
	ou/ow diphthongs	22
	oi/oy diphthongs	23
	au/aw digraphs	24
	/*aw*/ pattern with *ough* and *oa*	25
R-Controlled Vowels	r-controlled vowels with *ar*	26
	long *a* patterns with *are*	27
	long *a* patterns with *air* and *ear*	28
	r-controlled vowels with *or*	29
	r-controlled vowels with *oar, oor, our, ore*	30
	r-controlled vowels with *quar, war, wor*	31
	r-controlled vowels with *er*	32
	r-controlled vowels with *ur*	33
	r-controlled vowels with *ear* and *ir*	34

Digital Resources

Accessing the Digital Resources

The digital resources can be downloaded by following these steps:

1. Go to **www.tcmpub.com/digital**

2. Sign in or create an account.

3. Click **Redeem Content** and enter the ISBN number, located on page 2 and the back cover, into the appropriate field on the website.

4. Respond to the prompts using the book to view your account and available digital content.

5. Choose the digital resources you would like to download. You can download all the files at once, or you can download a specific group of files.

ISBN:
9781425833114

Please note: Some files provided for download have large file sizes. Download times for these larger files will vary based on your download speed.

 ## Contents of the Digital Resources

Teaching Resources Folder

- Additional Spelling Activities (page 7)

- Additional Word Lists (below, on, and above grade level)

- Unit Overview Pages

Assessments Folder

- Analysis Charts separated by spelling category

- Unit Assessments (pages 237–238)

- Assessment Reproducible
